TOO
MUCH

Cindy Lee Neighbors, MD

Published by CLN Publishing LLC, Honolulu, Hawaii

www.cindyleeneighbors.com

ISBN: 979-8-89034-160-0 (Paperback)
       979-8-89034-162-4 (Hardcover)
       979-8-89034-161-7 (eBook)

Disclaimer: The views expressed in this book are those of the author and do not necessarily reflect the official policy or position of the Department of Defense or the U.S. Government.

Glossary: A glossary of terms is included at the end of this book for reference; however, it may contain *spoilers*

Library of Congress Control Number: 2023907811

Printed in the United States of America

First Edition

for my bffs.

CHAPTER 1

Freedoms

This is better than jail or a psych ward—is what I tell myself.

Some people would kill for this life.

A life on the beach.

Endless rolling waves crash white foam against blankets of crisp, tan sand. I have it all to myself. *I'm not grateful.*

Nearly every morning the sunlight hits the water just right to make it illuminate like fresh blown glass, and in those moments, I could choose to be grateful.

Been told, "I choose to smile." But I just can't. It feels like I'm stranded on a deserted island. *Nobody is coming.*

It's July 2023. I'm in Hawaii. Still considered the United States. Technically, I have freedoms. I should be free. I've tried to kill myself. So why is someone like me, in a little piece of heaven, so damn miserable? Why do I feel like a prisoner in paradise? And how is it that I'm a licensed physician…living on a remote beach?

I'd be lying if I said I planned this out. This was never in my wildest dreams, a dream of mine at all.

Going to medical school was never something I dreamed of when I was a child.

It sounds entitled, I'm sure.

But it happened—this story. And here I am.

Stuck on a beach.

Watching the waves roll in and out.

Sending emails and emails. Trying to escape. From what appears to be one of the most beautiful spots in a first world country. Racing to publish my story.

Because the truth is, I'm not completely innocent. I'm not guilty either. I've tried to die. Fantasized the different ways I could leave and never come back. Contemplated many other terribly violent things.

What if I'm a bad person? Do I deserve this beautiful life?

As a doctor, the thought of surviving a suicide attempt aborted my plans. For example, jumping from a building. With my luck, I imagined I'd survive and become paraplegic. From a hanging, maybe need a tracheostomy. Gunshot wound, facial reconstruction surgery. And so on.

I'd just end up in some more horrific life than whatever it was that I was running away from.

And then I realized, the perfect solution, would actually be faking my own death.

That's what I'd fantasize about at work.

As a writer, I'd come up with the most epic plots.

How could I possibly fake my own death, save up enough money, adopt a whole new identity and just…run away? It seemed impossible…yet there was a glimmer of hope in my imagination. As a daughter, sister, friend, student, and lover, it felt selfish.

But I stopped caring about everybody else.

I needed to be free.

* * *

When I was encouraged to attend military medical school because it was "free," I forgot what I learned in sixth grade: "there is no such thing as a free lunch."

* * *

Before med school, I was an aspiring actress. My acting coach reminded us that "luck is when opportunity meets preparation." But I wasn't so lucky after I graduated from USC. I needed to make money to pay rent because my parents had cut me off. Got a job at an Optometry clinic within walking distance of my apartment. Interacting with patients was the best part. *Grey's Anatomy* made the life of a surgeon seem so glamorous and sexy. As a theatre major, my studies focused on everything but science. I researched "how to get into med school." Signed up for premed community college courses. Studied for the MCAT.

There were days in residency and med school where I'd search my actor friends and classmates online. The ones who didn't quit seemed to be making it.

There were days I wish I didn't quit acting.

But this story isn't about my failure trying to become an actress.

This story is about my failure becoming a board-certified Otolaryngology Head and Neck Surgeon.

* * *

The waves crash back and forth. Sometimes they soothe me to sleep. Sometimes I'm wired—up all night—in my manic state. Pacing and pacing around, like a hamster. Peeking out the balcony door into the dark night. Whipping open my laptop to fire off another deranged email.

No.

No more emails.

Sending emails and texts without thinking is what got me here—and here isn't where I want to be. I'm stuck in a never-ending loophole. I just want to break free.

Freedoms

The sun is rising and a beach pigeon lands on my balcony. It stares at me as if it wants something, and even this bird is freer than I'll ever be—but I worry—*is it happy?*

I'm sick of being told that "perception is reality."

Why can't reality be reality? What if looks *are* deceiving?

People don't go through years of surgical residency only to end up stranded on a beach, to lose their mind. 37 years old. No house. No family. No job.

Trapped inside a hamster wheel with my computer. I don't have enough money to fake my own death and run away. Knowing my luck, I'd get caught.

And I don't want to end up in jail...*for trying to be free?*

For now, I have to settle for *this...*

Some people will say this book is for vengeance. Some will say that I'm too crazy to be credible. But if I'm credible, is it so bad to be honest?

CHAPTER 2

Stories

This story isn't like most stories. It's a true story. I'm not anonymous, so it's a little risky. Believe what you want. If it makes everyone feel better, let's not call it "a true story." You're wondering—how and why did someone so psychotic manage to get into the military?

By the way—I wasn't always crazy. But I promise to do my best telling you everything I can without flying off the handle. Or at least, "be normal." Just like you, I want the truth.

It all started with my plan to become a doctor—a surgeon…in the United States Army.

* * *

February 2014, Honduras

SELFIE of me trying not to complain (even though the rucksack is kind of killing me)

trekking my best life through the jungle in camos

> *location untagged*
> #NoFilter #No #More #Selfies

Two years into med school, I joined a reconnaissance mission trip in Honduras. The 98-degree heat was oppressive, and the "toilets" were non-flushable pits. Not your typical med school experience—a new-found sense of adventure. I snapped away, documenting the novelty of it all.

My motivations weren't entirely altruistic. Honduras was a resume builder—primarily. An added bonus of clean-cut, muscular soldiers in the background. One night, fueled by alcohol and camaraderie in a dimly lit bar, I'm belting out Madonna's "Like a Virgin" with two of these Ken soldiers. What started as innocent fun quickly escalated into a three-hour karaoke session, a blur of 80s and 90s hits.

Alcohol made dancing with strange men in a foreign place seem not so strange. This made it easy to fall back into the art of pretending. To numb with meaningless sex and booze. Telling myself that the inequalities I was blind to were just illusions.

People are born lucky or unlucky. And nobody really knows the difference anyway. At the end of the day, all of our shit ends up in the same place, somehow. Somewhere. Yet, even as I danced and laughed and lost myself in the magic, a quiet voice kept me from slipping too far. It reminded me that all escapes are fleeting. This stolen joy was not real. Home, filled with my hidden demons, still haunted me from halfway across the world.

* * *

March 2014, Military Medical School, Bethesda, Maryland

The karaoke high wore off as quickly as it came, leaving me with a familiar emptiness. "America's Med School," also known as the Military Medical School. It's across the street from the National Institutes of Health in Bethesda, Maryland. Walking across the picturesque brick campus in my Army dress blues, I was living the American Dream. We earn our tuition through service, trading a commitment to the military after graduation.

Graduating from med school debt-free would be a golden ticket. On interview day, the slideshow flashed tempting images like international mission trips and the iconic flamingo-pink hospital perched on the hill above my childhood home.

I was sold—like a sucker at a timeshare presentation.

Growing up, my dad always had the news on TV. I'd beg him to turn it off, sparking heated contention. The stories seemed too horrific to be true or perhaps not quite believable enough. I grew weary of the constant negativity and eventually disconnected from current events entirely.

Joining the Army in exchange for "free med school" was beyond ironic. Nothing could be more real. Until I met Paul, the man who changed my life. My world came crashing down around me like an existential crisis. Not the day I met him—the moment I fell in love. It happened during one of our military medicine lectures, of all places. Yes, it sounds crazy. Because it is. For some reason, our entire class was subjected to watching the film *Restrepo*—an American documentary about the 173rd Airborne Brigade Combat Team in the Korengal Valley of Afghanistan.

A mere glimpse into the sacrifice, pain, and complexity of these soldiers' experiences was deeply unsettling. When the film ended, the darkened auditorium fell silent for a few seconds as we collectively caught our breath. The room smelled of stale carpet and men's deodorant mixed with chewing gum.

When the lights flickered on, a handsome blonde man was standing at the podium. Paul. One of the most decorated officers in our school, he was a West Point graduate who went on to serve in the infantry—before deciding to become an Army doctor, like the rest of us.

His brown eyes glistened as he cleared his throat. "The people in the film who came in at the end," he began, his voice thick with emotion, "that was my platoon. What you saw was true. We were in a firefight every single day. You would hear mortars and rounds of gunfire all night, all day. For nine months, we were there."

I leaned forward, hanging onto every word. A strange warmth spread through me, a mix of admiration and an unfamiliar stirring in my heart. I noticed the way his hands gripped the podium, the slight tremor in his voice, the intensity in his eyes. This was a man who had seen and experienced things I could barely fathom. And after all that, he chose to continue dedicating his life to others.

When he finished speaking, a hush fell over the auditorium. I glanced around, some classmates stunned, others unfazed—nobody else, enthralled—like me. I couldn't look away from Paul. In that moment, something shifted within me. The stirrings of a feeling that would consume me, something that would control my every thought, decision, and action, something I would later come to understand as…love.

I had never met anyone like Paul. *People like him exist outside the movies.* Fighting for their lives. In places people don't talk about.

Guilt, shame, anger, and despair washed over me. What if everything I had ever learned about the world was a carefully constructed illusion? I had grown up sheltered, privileged, protected from the harsh realities of life. Was this a blessing or a curse?

In that auditorium, I began to feel things for Paul that I still can't fully comprehend. When he sat down, no one spoke. In the still silence, I could sense Paul's pain, love, and passion all at once. Above all, I felt an overwhelming admiration, a feeling that would carry me through everything that was to follow.

Pathology lab partnership bloomed into study sessions. Paul would quiz me from across the table, seemingly impressed when I aced difficult questions. Sometimes, I admit, I would study even harder just to earn his approval. Created guides using rainbow pens, studying trivial facts—chemical life-cycles and microscopic things.

From high school to college, subtly manipulating men became a special forte. In LA, dating meant self-tanner, fake eyelashes, acrylic nails, and frantically rehearsing lines for auditions. In med school, the same skill set translated to memorizing the histopathology of thyroid cancers and the physiology of renal diseases.

Both Paul and I joined the Army to make a difference, to build stable, lucrative careers. When he started reciprocating my attention, it felt validating. He saw my knowledge and skills, not just superficial attributes. Paul was a breath of fresh air, even though he secretly nicknamed me "Barbie in the Army." It seemed he could appreciate a smart girl who'd play pretend, so I put in extra effort on days we had labs and study sessions.

Could Paul be my Soldier Ken Doll?

* * *

March 2016, San Antonio, Texas

Fast forward two years. Paul and I were in Texas for clinical rotations, sharing a cramped room in a rundown house we found online. Our relationship intensified quickly, bordering on obsession. In our minds, it was kept secret from our classmates. We had no choice—because technically, he was still married.

Late at night, messy, in sweaty sheets, the air thick with the heat. Paul would absently trace patterns on my foot as he recounted his harrowing experiences in Afghanistan. How he killed dozens of people, yet brushed off any suggestion of PTSD. Before his second deployment, he confessed that he switched from infantry to the medical corps because he felt guilty about his first—driven by a desire to save the lives he'd once been trained to take. He talked about the civilians his unit took care of—

"I don't get it…the Army would take care of people they accidentally injured?" I asked, so naïve, so oblivious.

"Yeah—I mean—shit happens," he'd brush it off.

Paul was a real-life war hero. I was captivated by his stories, desperate to understand his past. To psychoanalyze…if he could ever recover from a war that he claimed didn't traumatize him. I felt bad that I hadn't followed the news. Paul already lived a whole other life.

The Texas heat was stifling, even at night. The air conditioner sputtered. Paul lay beside me, his chest rising and falling with each breath underneath the faded jersey sheet, illuminated by the faint glow of the streetlight filtering through the blinds.

I traced the contours of his face with my fingertips, the rough stubble of his beard he'd have to shave first thing in the morning.

"Did you hate being deployed?" I asked.

Paul's eyes flickered open, his gaze meeting mine. A shadow of pain crossed his features, but it was quickly replaced by a stoic mask. "It was a long time ago," he said, his voice gruff.

"How many?" I asked, my fingers gently tracing his forehead. "You know you can tell me anything."

He sighed, turning to face me. "Let's not talk about it."

"Did you see them die?" My voice filled with a longing to bridge the distance between us. "I won't judge you, Paul. I accept you and your past."

I probed. "Anyone from your unit?"

"Not when I was deployed," he admitted, letting out a sigh.

"What do you mean?" I said, my heart pounding.

He sighed again and reached for a glass of water. "Two of my guys killed themselves when we came back. And then there was Natasha. She was murdered four years ago."

"Murdered?" I whispered.

"They convicted him last summer," his voice lowered.

He continued, "I had to call her parents. I knew—that something was wrong—that morning…she didn't show up for formation. The guy—it was the guy she left with. We—we helped search for her body."

Paul described his duties as the commander, filing reports, contacting family members. Searching for her body in the woods. He was grief stricken, and I tried to focus on his words, but I could barely pay attention. I was gripped with my own questions—how they couldn't find her body—how it took years to find the murderer—to find her body.

In the days that followed, Natasha's murder haunted my thoughts. I couldn't shake the image of her life cut short, the unanswered questions swirling around her death. I was triggered.

Late at night, when Paul was asleep, I found myself obsessively researching the case, digging into news articles. Started sleuthing on the internet. Found a family support group online. *Why it took so long… to find her body…to find who did it…to convict the guy.*

I knew it was irrational, but the seed of doubt had been planted, and it grew with every sleepless night…A dark and twisted thought took root in my mind, a thought I would never say out loud: *What if Paul had something to do with it?*

I think it makes sense that I was starting to get paranoid. Paul's marriage was a topic we navigated carefully, but as we grew more serious, having to keep our relationship a secret bothered me more and more. It was almost impossible to hide from our classmates.

People knew about "us." But acted like they didn't. He went on an underground campaign to let our friends know that he was in the process of a divorce. Walking through the hallways at school, it seemed like our classmates would look down when I walked by. I could feel my heart wanting to rip out of my chest. I could hear my eardrums pounding out of my head.

Whispers and sideways glances fueled my paranoia. I was the "home-wrecker," an outsider caught in a web of deceit. The weight of guilt, and fear, pressed down on me, a constant reminder of the potential consequences of our choices.

One hot, sweaty evening in bed, Paul dropped a bombshell: his soon-to-be-ex-wife was threatening to file charges against him.

"Charges for what?"

"It's not a big deal."

"You didn't answer my question."

Paul said nothing. Maybe he was remembering something difficult, or figuring out a way to spin the truth. It was our first argument. You know how couples never forget their first argument—this one is forever drilled into my memory.

"I went out for cigarettes one night when we were still living in North Carolina. It was December, just before Christmas."

"You smoked?" I didn't care so much about the smoking. I just needed to distract myself from what I feared was the truth—*Paul wasn't the perfect man I envisioned. The red flags had arrived.* I needed anything to distract me from them.

"She tried to stop me from going. I went to my car, but she had my keys, and she yelled at me to come back inside. Next thing I know, I'm in the house, and she's cut the bottom of her foot on a broken wineglass"— he paused and swallowed—"I was too drunk to drive. She claimed that I hit her and sprained her ankle. But I didn't."

I ignored the phantom wine glass detail. I ignored the drunkenness. Instead, I tried to be practical. "Was there a police report?"

"No."

"Did you go to the emergency room with her?"

Paul shook his head.

"Do you want to go back to her?"

His wife hadn't signed the papers. My biggest fear was that I'd gotten my hopes up—what if she wanted him back? That this allegation was just some ploy to get him back.

TOO MUCH

What if I had become too infatuated —obsessed—with Paul...and I couldn't let go?

"I sent her some money just now, so hopefully she will sign," he tapped at his phone.

Something about the story didn't add up. *Why was a fight from years ago coming up now? What if his ex knew about me and wanted to retaliate as much as she could to ruin his reputation and our relationship?*

I reasoned with myself that eventually I could crack the truth. But I didn't have her version—only his. Whether Paul was guilty or not guilty all that time ago, I carried secondhand culpability around with me.

I started to believe that someday, it'd catch up to me somehow. Karma for stealing another woman's man. I worked to convince myself I didn't steal him. And so did Paul.

Over and over again, he'd say, "I was getting divorced before we started dating. I'm not leaving her for you."

No matter how many times he'd say it, I couldn't believe him.

The question would always remain: *Why now?*

Paul painted a picture of himself as a suffering and misunderstood husband, trapped in a dead relationship. A soon-to-be-ex-wife is a convenient villain.

Paul was this heroic officer from West Point. Soon to be doctor. Honorable. Easy on the eyes. Put Paul in a pair of faded jeans, hand him a golden retriever puppy, and wrap him up in Old Glory. He was, simply, the kind of all American guy most would be happy to introduce to the parents.

My obsessive love convinced me that we were meant to be together. If anything, to be grateful. To love him more, love him better, like he deserved. Red flags and suspected PTSD aside, Paul really was the picture-perfect husband I always wanted.

A second marriage fresh after divorce seemed extreme, but to boost our chances of matching into the same residency after graduating, it felt like a necessary evil. All the other couples in our class were doing it—getting married to match together.

It didn't seem like a big deal. I told myself that marriage was just a piece of paper. Just a formality. After Texas, we traveled to Hawaii, my home state, for surgical rotations. I gave Paul an ultimatum.

His first failed marriage didn't have to be a dealbreaker. Paul and I had until the military residency match in December—nine more months—to put his past behind us. I told myself that his wife's threats weren't real—looked the other way every time his phone vibrated. There was no possible way he'd ever be charged with a crime. He was studying to become a doctor. He was honorable. Serving.

It sounds crazy, but I told myself that if Paul didn't kill his missing soldier, he didn't abuse his ex-wife. I told myself what I wanted to believe.

That should have been good enough...right?

TOO MUCH

* * *

July 2016, Karaoke Bar, Hawaii

Paul and I spent the next three months on clinical rotations in Hawaii at Main Hospital. Three solid months of barely sleeping and re-caffeinating to fuel the sex romps that we squeezed in between memorizing anatomy for surgical cases. I was in my hometown, but I didn't see my friends or family once. Paul and I barely saw each other. Yet, we were madly in love.

One humid summer night, Paul and I were invited to late night Karaoke in Waikiki. It was hardcore like a college throwback. The partying blurred into an early morning of Soju shots and drunken singing. Surgical residents flashing pics from the most gruesome cases of the week.

"Check out this guy's foot. Hacked off with a machete!" One of them sloshed towards me. Paul and I were getting our first real taste of this mysterious, high-stakes, high-adrenaline world, and we wanted all of it.

During the week, when I discovered a moment of gold in the OR—like identifying anatomy correctly, it gave me a rush like no other. After hours and hours of retracting, standing like a statue, watching miraculous work, I longed to hear the words, "Cindy, you can close."

Being part of the dance in the operating room fueled my insatiable curiosity. The surgeons meticulously and artfully removed tissues, layer by layer. Without looking up from the surgical field, they'd pass their instruments—suctioning here, cauterizing there, ever so effort-lessly and delicately.

Smoke plume filled up the surgical field as one dissected around ves-sels and nerves, while the other suctioned blood. My job as the au-ditioning med stud was to remain silent and still. Do whatever I was told, for however long it took.

Twenty-eight hours was my longest surgery. We scrubbed out for bathroom and snack breaks. If the top 100 wasn't playing, the anes-thesia monitors beeping and hissing kept us awake. The freezing, cold days in the OR could be long, but never boring.

Being in the OR was like being in the presence of gods, and suturing was just a treat. But the most rewarding part of it all turned out to be something I hadn't expected. Because it didn't have anything to do with operating…

Mr. A was a patient with squamous cell carcinoma of the tongue. He lived on another island with difficult access to an ENT. Diagnosed late, his prognosis was poor. By the time he sought a second opinion, the mass was eroding through his cheek and lip and the cancer had metastasized to his neck and lungs.

Main Hospital was all about MRB, "Maximum Resident Benefit," which meant doing everything we could for the sake of learning. We resected Mr. A's affected cheek, lip, and bilateral neck lymph nodes. Months later, he underwent chemoradiotherapy.

Desperate and full of magical thinking when faced with a terminal di-agnosis, families say "yes" to it all, out of love or denial or both. Even if the patient is ready to let go. Mr. A had a very lovely wife. One day she stopped me and my senior resident, in the cafeteria. She asked, "how long he had left."

We had just talked about it at tumor board. But neither of us had the heart—or expertise to discuss it in such great detail. The unvarnished truth was that chemorads, a final desperate measure, would only grant Mr. A, an unknowable, finite, amount of time.

It took me years to fully appreciate that, in spite of experience, in spite of job title, nobody ever really knows how long someone has "left." Even if we kind of knew, we didn't. Sometimes people live longer than expected. Sometimes not. Nothing is guaranteed.

Doctors—surgeons—are not gods. But doctors aspire to be gods.

Cynical to state the obvious—we can't change fate. It's a fallacy to think that we can conquer death. The belief makes some of us feel like gods. The power lies in the perceived ability to control the circumstances about which we can create an illusion such that time can be manipulated.

For better or worse, mortality is inevitable. Knowing the truth behind the scenes—the secrets, the deceit, the mastery of it all—might be the best part.

Nothing to do with the art of medicine, and everything to do with control. Not many people will admit that, of course. It's a secret. And nobody else willingly talks about the drugs, the alcohol. The blurry Karaoke nights. How something about numbing all of the pain in between the highs and the lows of the chaos of that world has a comforting effect.

Sounds a little sadistic, doesn't it?

What I fear that I loved most about this dark world is that as much as it seemed like I was an outsider to the boy's club, I fit right in. The epic gory freakshow of residents griping, singing, boozing, and boasting reminded me of why I never belonged in a traditional sorority.

"I closed all by myself without the attending scrubbed in!"

Their world was the manic-depressive surgical rollercoaster I knew all too well. And yet, so seemingly cool and stable from the outsider's perspective.

Surgery wasn't just about money or career stability. It was an elite underground club—full of guts, glory, good-looking guys—and it was Really. Fucking. Cool.

I didn't just want to be part of it. I wanted it to be mine.

Drugs and alcohol had been my secret escape since I was a teen, following me to my college days, and if these people were okay with letting loose like this after insanely long days of working, finding ways to be their most authentic selves, maybe I had found a place I could genuinely call "home."

The thing about addiction is—it's a never-ending battle with myself. I had been relatively sober for probably a decade. Stable. Functional…

so I think back to this moment—*why there and then. Why did I have to love it so much? Did I just have to belong?*

It was perfect. Stumbling around in the dark, they were too drunk, too numb, too gifted, too beautiful, too stupid, and too fucking smart to care.

At the end of the day, I belonged there more than anywhere else. Not in my chaotic world trying to impress my family, desperate to dodge all the whispers, sick of deciphering the threats from Paul's ex, tired of sifting through his past life.

This dark, gritty world that the bigger world called "surgery," *this* could be my sanctuary...*maybe I could heal here...*I could secretly be nobody and somebody all at the same time.

Even if it was sadistic, so what?

As the karaoke lights swirled and the laughter echoed, maybe what I found was more than just a temporary escape—the thrills of chasing the highs and escaping my reality—what if it could be my secret? A home within my home.

* * *

October 2016, Bethesda, Maryland

After our Hawaii rotations, we were recalled to Bethesda as the crisp fall welcomed us. Paul made arrangements for us to go out to dinner at a fancy steakhouse.

Watching him spin circles to get ready, I suspected that he was going to propose. He was fussing around too much: fixing his tie, changing out his shoes, messing with his collar in the mirror.

I pretended everything was normal. Didn't see any sign of a ring in his jacket on our short walk over. Even so, I couldn't help myself from picking at my cuticles underneath the table. Our wine arrived. Paul whipped out a huge blue Ring Pop candy and grinned, "Cindy, will you marry me?"

"No." I smiled coyly, my heart squeezing in my throat.

"No? Okay, then!" He pulled out a beautiful rock of a diamond. "What about now?"

"Oh my gosh! Yes!"

I couldn't have been happier. In spite of our heated arguments, the legal issues, the drama with our travel, and all the late-night cramming sessions, I was still madly, deeply, in love with Paul—red flags included.

* * *

December 2017, Hawaii

A year later, Paul and I were deep into our engagement. The best Christmas present arrived: We matched into our respective surgical subspecialties at Main Hospital.

Paul matched into Urology and I matched into Otolaryngology.

TOO MUCH

We were going to be surgeons.

Gods in the making.

In Hawaii.

Paul's divorce finalized earlier that year so we could go public with our engagement. What more could we possibly ask for? We were accepted into two of the most competitive surgical subspecialties. Set to become DINKS!

Everything I ever wanted was within reach. My ring finger was weighed down with a massive rock, and I owned a high-rise condo overlooking the heart of up-and-coming Kaka'ako. A beautiful home. A job—a career that I could be proud of—finally—something worthwhile—something I could talk about with friends and family.

My perfect dream wedding was just around the corner.

All the things. Things I didn't have before Paul. All Instagram-worthy. I was going to be the success story I always dreamt of becoming. I could finally make my family proud. *Could I finally be happy?*

* * *

February 2017, Military Medical School, Bethesda, Maryland

Two months post-match, I was still riding the high of landing an ENT residency. Wedding planning consumed my days. Pinterest boards filled with visions of blogger-perfect island vintage aesthetic celebrations. We were back on campus for final exams, just a couple of

24

months away from starting our new lives in Hawaii. Every day felt like Friday afternoon, a giddy anticipation bubbling beneath the surface.

Paul and I were studying in the med student lounge when our classmate, Marvin, sauntered by, mocking my "Valley Girl" voice. "Let's go to the OR, guuuys. When are we, like, going to the OR!? Army Barbie wants to operate!"

I rolled my eyes, nearly spilling my lukewarm coffee. A flash of navy blue caught my attention. A high-ranking officer, dressed in his service uniform, approached our table, his eyes locked on Paul.

The air thickened, the laughter dying in my throat. A silent exchange passed between Paul and me, a flicker of fear in his eyes.

"Lieutenant Jackson?" the officer said, his voice low and authoritative.

"Paul—" I whispered, a knot forming in my stomach.

The officer gestured for Paul to stand. I rose too, my voice trembling. "What's going on?"

Paul avoided my gaze. "Cindy, I'll explain later."

But the officer cut him off. "Lieutenant Jackson, I'm Captain Green. Spoke to your company commander this morning. Taking you to MPD now to process charges for assault and battery," he said with his voice lowered, still intense and commanding.

Paul followed without a word, as if he already knew this was coming. Leaving me gutted. In the dark.

As if I had no idea. *I knew.* The ex-wife's abuse allegations. All the nights I had questioned Paul and he dodged around the truth. Telling me stories about the wine glass and the foot and the cigarettes.

I almost let myself forget. After our engagement and match, all that ugliness had faded away from my mind. And now it would never let me forget: Karma. In all of its disgusting glory.

My cell phone rang. Figuring she was calling about the wedding, flower arrangements. Something trivial. Robotically, I answered. After nearly four years studying to become a doctor and a wife for a life that was a dream, I felt so incredibly empty and lost in that brick-walled-institution I had learned to call home. Normally, I wouldn't have answered, but in that moment, more than ever before, I was grateful for my—

"Dad's in the ICU," my mom cried.

Every day feeling like a Friday afternoon was too good to be true.

CHAPTER 3

Echoes

March 2017, Oahu Medical Center, Hawaii

How quickly he had deteriorated. His papery skin stretched across his sharp cheekbones. His facial hair had faded to a pasty white since the last time I saw him. Dad looked older. Deeply unwell. One thing was familiar: his left arm darker than the right—speckled with sun spots.

Decades ago, he had a habit of hanging his left arm out of his 1970s Monte Carlo—a car that embarrassed me because it was old and purple. On our long drives home from school, he'd swing out his arm, tossing empty soda cans and cigarette butts into the gutters. I believed a magical recycling center existed beneath our world, collecting the litter as we drove home. Only later did I realize it was draining into the ocean.

I'd ask to be picked up late from school, when the sun set—so other kids wouldn't see him. He was a lot older than the other dads. Twenty-five years older than my mom. I always thought people were looking at the car—not my parents' age gap.

All those memories felt like a lifetime ago as I sat beside my father's hospital bed, the sterile scent of antiseptic heavy in the air. I wished we could go cruising around in his purple Monte Carlo, the golden afternoon sun painting his skin. I wouldn't care what anyone was thinking. I knew that in spite of his shortcomings, my father was a good man. Maybe this is why I believed Paul was good, too.

As I witnessed it, my parents spent most of their marriage fighting. Fighting about money. And the hardship to provide my brother and me with a good education in one of the most affluent places in the world. I didn't dare invite my friends or classmates over after school— they had much nicer homes than I could ever dream of. My family was anything but wealthy. The half-built house where we grew up— faded light green paint peeling from its sun-baked exterior, mounted on stilts above a makeshift foundation of rocks and cinderblocks— was a touchpoint for Mom's anger for as long as I can remember. We all learned to walk lightly around Lynn.

Lynn is my mother's Americanized name. She moved to Hawaii after graduating from college in the Philippines. I never understood it— the story seemed much different than what I put together as an adult. "Write me a check! Write me a check!" Lynn would yell. Threatening to leave my father on a weekly basis if he didn't write her a check. Packing and unpacking her suitcases like clockwork. Except this family ritual involved lots of screaming, crying, door slamming, and the endless shuffling of luggage. Her eyes darted around violently, her face wrinkling into a grimace, her silky black hair fanning out over her shoulders.

As dysfunctional as my parents were, they managed to run an office from home, the kitchen table overflowing with invoices. It was a complex work-marriage relationship I never quite understood. Lynn would type up Dad's invoices, and Dad would deliver OBGYN supplies to doctors around the island. He'd take me on deliveries, windows down, the wind whipping through my hair, repugnant cigarette smoke suffocating me. The Beach Boys or The Beatles always playing. Back then, the nurses and doctors would say I was cute. I'd smile as we offered them mangoes from our tree.

I loved watching my parents. To me, it was like watching them run a secret mission. Sometimes I'd answer the phone when they were busy.

"Hi, this is Lynn with Moxi Medical, how can I help you?" I'd say doing my best Lynn impersonation. Started "working" for fun when I was nine years old. Lynn would spend countless hours perfecting the invoices and organizing all the medical supplies in the overflowing boxes—all things assuredly that my father couldn't do on his own. If my father didn't "write her a check", she'd get mad. I secretly played on the typewriter, my fingers mimicking hers. Trying to decipher the faint impressions left on used pages, curious about what she typed. I can still remember the clicking sounds, the smell of my dad's cigarettes, the creaks of the floor as my parents scurried around. It was ghetto. And fabulous.

* * *

March 2017, Main Hospital, Hawaii

Radiology was an elective, a welcome respite with shorter hours that allowed me to visit my ailing father. It was one of my final rotations as a medical student at Main Hospital, the same place I'd be starting residency in a few short months. Every now and then, I'd be invited to scrub in on surgeries—opportunities I couldn't refuse.

That's how I met Dr. Thatcher, a handsome visiting surgeon who didn't permanently practice at Main. He had a soft Southern accent and spoke like a gentleman, unexpected for a surgeon. He wore thick glasses, but they didn't hide his piercing blue eyes. Despite being engaged to Paul, I couldn't help but notice Dr. Thatcher's flirtatious attention. He would strike up conversations, his eyes lingering a little too long. One day, he invited me for coffee.

I opened up to him about my father's illness, the complications in my relationship with Paul. It was probably an overshare. While I wasn't necessarily attracted to Dr. Thatcher, his attention was flattering, a distraction from the mounting stress in my life.

He was married, a surgeon, and I was engaged. It felt wrong. Yet, there was a part of me that craved the validation, the escape from the impending storm that my life was becoming.

* * *

March 2017, Oahu Medical Center, Hawaii

Lynn hit me with it as soon as I entered the sterile room. "You need to do something, Cindy," she said. Her eyes baggy, wrinkled, aged. My mother used to be so pretty and young. Now, she looked like a grandmother, which made me feel even more guilty because I didn't have any plans to have children of my own.

The chaos within her mirrored what was stirring within me. Paul's legal troubles mixed with my bougie wedding plans were draining our finances—and now this. Dad's diagnosis was a real-life terror: end-stage renal disease, complicated by an ischemic stroke. Conditions and concepts I once brain-dumped could turn our lives into a raging dumpster fire.

Echoes

Lynn paced the room. Her eyes darting from me to my dad, searching for a miracle. She shuffled to the nurses' station for more blankets, speaking in rapid-fire Tagalog. Sending high-pitched laughs and screeches echoing down the hall. A circus of mixed emotions.

Dr. Allen, a boomer attending from an ICU rotation, appeared at my side. "I'm sorry to see you under these circumstances," he said, his voice a mix of sympathy and professionalism.

"What do you think?" I asked, my voice barely a whisper.

He glanced at the monitor displaying Dad's vitals, then met my gaze. "Your father has two options: to start dialysis or go to hospice."

"How long would he be in hospice?" *A question I immediately resented asking—as if he knew.*

"It's hard to say, we really—"

"I need to know." And yet—I insisted that this situation was different. That my dad had an expiration date and his doctor would know.

"Probably three to six months."

He was "full code." But I needed to hear it from my dad. I combed through his chart, desperately searching for the miracle my mom couldn't find. And then, like a pit in my stomach—was he ready to die?

As if it was a choice.

And like a magician of sorts, Dr. Allen leaned over to say, "People think life is an all-you-can-eat buffet...you have to make choices, prioritize what truly matters."

I looked at my father, his eyes closed, his breaths shallow and labored.

Was he suffering? Would he rather be here...or wherever we go next? Was there anything else he wanted to do? Would there be enough time? Did we do enough together? Was he proud of me?

Did he have a good life?

The questions gnawed at me. The guilt and pain from some of our car rides resurfaced—my earliest memories of a secret side of Cindy that only my father really knew. Sometimes Paul saw it. Otherwise, the real Cindy was hiding from the rest of the world—*Crazy Cindy.*

In those car rides, I could be mean.

"I'm going to throw away your cigarettes," I'd yell. I'd yell at him not just about the news. But as I got older, many things. The news. His car. The house. Maybe, it stemmed from watching the way Lynn wildly erupted...All this pent-up rage inside me, how sometimes, I was so mad. And I blamed my father for it. For being old. For having a purple car. For not finishing the house. For things that—ultimately, I came to learn, he couldn't quite control. Not all of it. And then the times, I would throw his cigarettes away. After all these years, the irony, with him dying from end-stage renal disease, I felt guilty for throwing his cigarettes away. For yelling at him to quit smoking.

I sat there, rubbing the flakes of dead skin off his darkened arm, wishing he would open his eyes so I could ask for his forgiveness. If he still loved me.

* * *

1990s, Hawaii

Kyle is my younger brother. He and I were best friends growing up. We'd play around the house, in the gravel, and around the mango tree. Our parents picking hundreds of mangoes, sticky and sweet. We didn't have a fancy treehouse, but we had enough space to pretend. Hiding little toys and journals inside the cinderblocks.

This was when Nintendo and video games first became popular. Kyle was much better than me at Mortal Kombat, our favorite game, but I'd play along anyway. He'd always win.

Now he's really into video games, part of a whole streaming community. They sit and talk all day, playing as if their lives depend on it. I guess for some of them, it does. I asked my brother if he's a secret streamer, but he denies it, saying it's too late to start monetizing. He just plays for fun.

* * *

April 2017, Oahu Medical Center, Hawaii

"Did you review his charts?" my mother asked. "What can you do?"

"I—I don't know—"

TOO MUCH

"How can you not know? You went to medical school."

Although I hadn't eaten all day, I wasn't hungry. I was about to graduate from medical school. Accepted into a competitive surgical residency. But I still failed my family. Swallowing the lump in my throat,
I texted Paul to stop myself from crying. Maybe his defense case was
dismissed. I hated feeling like a teenager again. Defensive and angry.

"I *do* know," I said, a bit too loudly.

Mom sat back in the visitor chair and crossed her arms.

"I do know, but—"

"But what?"

"But you're not going to like it." I recommended and explained DNR/DNI.

"Absolutely not," she growled, leaning over dad's body like he was
a deflated balloon, a possession. A DNR or DNI suggested that we
were giving up. "You need to get us into Side's Hospital."

"Side's?"

"They have better doctors there."

"I don't know if he can go to Side's. We might be able to get him
into hospice—"

"Hospice? Absolutely not."

Echoes

My father stirred. "I want to go home," he said. "Home-home."

Mom waved the suggestion away. "We want to go to Side's."

Dad didn't seem to want more treatment. Mom wanted it all. Feeling defeated, I went back to Dr. Allen to beg for a transfer to Side's.

When I was ten years old, my mom took off for real. Lynn spent a year or two as a flight attendant across the country. Leaving my brother and me to raise ourselves with our dad at home-home. Now I understand that she probably wanted to make money and have a life of her own. Even though she came back, things between us were never quite the same.

* * *

April 2017, Side's Hospital, Hawaii

Paul finally arrived in Hawaii, a long-awaited meeting with my dad overshadowed by the devastating news of his impending court-martial. Our wedding was a month away, but the prospect of a dishonorable discharge hung heavy in the air. He didn't want me at the trial, his empty eyes mirroring my own despair as we walked back into the hospital, a hollow shell of a couple.

Later, we sought solace in a Waikiki bar, drowning our anxieties in overpriced drinks. In a moment of drunken generosity, Paul insisted on buying me a designer bag, a gesture that felt both extravagant and desperate.

"Why now?" I asked, the weight of his words sinking in.

"Because... I don't know if I'll ever be able to in the future," he admitted, his voice thick with unspoken fears.

The $1800 price tag was a splurge I suspected we couldn't afford, with all the legal fees and wedding expenses looming around the corner. But in that moment of shared grief and uncertainty, acting on impulse gave us a rush of fleeting happiness. The bag, a beautiful yet ultimately meaningless object, would later become a haunting reminder of things beyond our means—things we didn't keep—things we didn't even need.

* * *

April 2017, Hospice, Hawaii

A week after getting into Side's, my father's condition deteriorated. He was diagnosed with aspiration pneumonia, further complicating his kidney failure. Each breath became a struggle as his lungs filled with fluid, the fight for survival growing tougher with each passing day. His prognosis was grim, with less than three months to live. We made the difficult decision to transfer him to hospice. Lynn was in denial about what hospice meant.

The hospice facility itself was worn and shabby, the linoleum floors scuffed, the windowsills thick with dust. Dad's shared room was crowded with three other patients, all waiting for the inevitable. He still wanted to go "home-home," but nobody felt comfortable with him dying there—nobody except me.

My mother and I would fight about it on the phone at night. I offered to take care of him, but who would give his medications, his tube feedings during the day when I was gone, she asked. After relenting, we tried it for a few days. It was a devastating failure. Dad was able to go home-home, for one last time. And then he returned back to hospice. I was crushed. I couldn't control when or how he died. He wanted to choose where he died, and I felt like I had failed him.

Inside Dad's room, Mom ignored Paul, her eyes fixed on me with a desperate plea. "I don't want him to die like this. Not like this," she whispered, her grip tightening on my hand. As if I could control how my father died.

I hadn't even graduated from med school, yet I felt the weight of playing God. I thought of Mrs. A, asking about her husband's prognosis. How I wish I could have told her that we can't control when or how people die.

Paul retreated to a corner, his presence a silent question mark. I yearned for his support, but he was battling his own demons. I had finally talked to my dad about changing his code status to DNR/DNI, and he agreed, multiple times, in moments of lucidity. A small comfort, but it didn't ease the ache in my heart.

Selfishly, I wondered what this unfolding tragedy would do to my own mental health, the energy I was banking to fight Paul's case. To walk myself at the wedding. Even though we'd hurried to plan it in just three weeks, hoping Dad would be there.

At least Dad knew that I had secured that coveted residency spot. He'd die believing that Paul was on the path to becoming a Urologist. Dad looked at Paul with a deep, serious gaze, then raised his arm in a weak wave. Paul waved back with a genuine smile. It was a fleeting moment of connection, a silent understanding passing between them.

As I sat beside Dad, holding his hand, Paul drifted over. Mom hovered nearby, her eyes filled with a mix of anger, fear, and grief. This wasn't like the time Mom left when we were kids, disappearing into the sky as a flight attendant.

Lynn stood over Dad's body, wailing, "Save Dad!"

Even though there was a DNR in place, she panicked. Dad's heart monitor beeped, the rhythm slowing, faltering. The machines hissed and whirred, but his breaths grew shallow, the spaces between them widening. The room felt heavy, the air thick with the impending finality.

The heart monitor flatlined. Silence.

My mother turned to me, her eyes wide with terror. "You killed him!"

I had no words. I had fought for his dignity, for a peaceful end. How could she not see that? How could she blame me?

The guilt twisted in my gut, a familiar ache echoing from childhood. To this day, the moment of his death is forever interwoven with her accusation. The doctor, the daughter, the murderer.

* * *

Mom had sent me a cell phone video just before Dad died. She sang to him, "Daddy, do you know how much I love you? Daddy, I love you. Do you know how much?"

"Too much," he whispered.

My mom loved him so much that it blinded her from seeing how letting him go was the right thing to do. Sometimes letting go is all we can do.

CHAPTER 4

Roses

April 2017, Hawaii

Red roses were his favorite—I never knew. Their heavy sweetness mingled with the tang of the salty Pacific breeze throughout the open church. Lynn ordered them herself. That's the only thing she could do that week.

"He wanted red roses," she sneered, "his favorite. He told *me* to order them."

That week Lynn was busy firing off emails to anyone who would read them, carefully crafting indictments against me. She was convinced he would have survived had it not been for the change in his code status. That it was my fault he died.

Paul was consumed by his looming court-martial. Legal phone calls filled every waking minute of his day, strategy sessions behind closed doors, emails and texts. I was left with all of the funeral arrangements—the caterer, the remembrance table, the drafting of eulogies, the invitations. It felt kind of manic with the frenzy. But the whirlwind of activity was a lifeline, a desperate attempt to drown out the heavy guilt and despair threatening to consume me.

Even so, with Lynn and her emails—she couldn't help herself. These emails she would fire off—it was back-and-forth between her and me. When she went, I would reply. Like a disgusting game with nobody winning.

Email
To: Les (the pastor who would be delivering the memorial)
From: Lynn
cc: Cindy and other family members
Subject: Roger
I'm still hurt by what happened to Roger. Cindy never gave him a chance to have hemodialysis. She insisted that Roger didn't want it, but Roger was confused, and I was supposed to make the decision. I don't think I can ever find closure to his death, and I don't think I can let go of the elderly, and her first victim was my husband.

I knew her grief was raw, her anger misplaced, but I was triggered. She didn't see the choices I had to make, out of love, out of respect for his wishes. That I wanted him to die with dignity. I didn't want his ribs crushed. I didn't want a team of nurses swarming around him in his last moments making last ditch efforts prolonging his life when it would be meaningless. Hooking him up to tubes and machines and lines and artificial things when it was time to let go. She couldn't see any of that because all she could see was a daughter who failed. I fired off nasty emails, and her responses only escalated.

It's your fault he is dead! Your fault, Cindy, and you know it! I will never forgive you, killer! Murderer!!! You cannot come here anymore. You hurt me so much to last a lifetime. It's irreparable and irreconcilable.

Then I couldn't help but wonder. Did I made a mistake? Should I have pushed harder for dialysis? Maybe my dad needed more information? What if he was scared? What if the dialysis was just something he didn't know anything about? The questions were a relentless chorus of self-recrimination.

I sent Lynn emails back. It was all I could do to reassure myself that I was right. Told her she was a bad mother. That I missed my father. That he was a better parent than her. I sent the emails she sent me to my family members. They didn't want to get involved. My friends suggested blocking her, so I tried. But Lynn would find new ways to send messages.

The day of the funeral arrived, a blur of black dresses and somber faces. Dr. Bates, my incoming program director, sat in the back of the church. I offered a small smile and he nodded at me, his tall presence an unsettling reminder of the professional responsibilities that awaited once I started my new life at Main. A life I wasn't even sure Paul would have. Paul was there physically, but mentally, in his own lost world, about to lose his entire career. I could tell he was trying to keep it together for me, but we snapped at each other earlier that morning.

Gracie, my steadfast rock in the storm, squeezed my hand as I delivered a eulogy that felt more like a confession. At the reception, Gracie pressed a new journal into my hands. "Write," she urged, her eyes filled with compassion. "Write it all down. It's the only way through."

I clutched the journal tightly, the sharp edges on my skin, a surprising comfort to the turmoil raging within. But as I stared at the empty pages, the memories flooded back, vivid and unrelenting. The scene of my father's final moments replayed in my mind's eye, the rasp of his breath, the fading light in his eyes... The words from Lynn, a web of pain too tight to unravel.

* * *

1996, *Private Elementary School, Hawaii*

Gracie and I were only ten years old when we first met. I had no idea she came from money. She had no idea I lived in a half-built house. None of that mattered at school. Neither of us had a global understanding of what our school really was—a simulation of sorts—an institution designed to protect us from the real world. Neither of us even grew up knowing the truth about each other—until adulthood—until now.

She was looking for a contact lens on the basketball courts outside at recess. Helpless and half-blind, I couldn't help but interrupt the boys playing to look for something smaller than our thumb on the dirty pavement. She frantically insisted her dad would "kill her" if she lost it, so we scrambled until – "Found it!" – the tiny, clear disc gleamed triumphantly on her fingertip. Then, like no big deal, she rinsed it off to pop back onto her eyeball.

A few weeks into 4th grade, we were inseparable. Insisted on having matching mini-backpacks and mini-journals. We'd hang around late in the afternoons together, relishing in "taking notes" about our surroundings, like *Harriet the Spy*. Her father dropped me off at home, just once. I didn't think they'd see the house. But one glance up at my parents' half-built home, leaning on cinderblocks, was all it took.

"Gracie, I don't want you coming back here," he said.

She didn't. But that didn't stop us from becoming best friends.

* * *

April 2017, Langley, Virginia

Only a week after cremating my father and sending off his ashes to be buried on the mainland, Paul was recalled to D.C. for his court-martial hearing. His entire career was on the line. Even though I'd just lost my dad, I wanted to be at Paul's side.

"I just want to do this by myself," he said. It felt like a slap in the face.

The gleaming wood-paneled Army courtroom was painted a cold white, the only decorations the crests of the Army and the United States. I dressed in a conservative black suit and tried to follow Paul and his lawyer into the room, but was stopped at the door. I found a seat in the back, just in time to hear Paul's mother on the stand, tears streaming down her face. "Nobody has ever loved my son the way he should be loved."

When the courtroom broke for recess, I tried to comfort Paul, but he pushed me away, his eyes cold. "Get out of here," he whispered. The heavy door sealed shut between us.

Trembling, I found a bench outside the courtroom. What didn't he want me to hear? An hour or two later, Paul and his lawyer emerged. They didn't even look at me as they headed to an adjacent office.

I followed, my heart pounding. Inside, our lawyer was sprawled on the floor, cursing. "Fuuuuuuck!"

We lost.

In the parking lot, Paul grabbed my arm, his grip tight and painful. "You shouldn't have been here. I lost because you came into that courtroom."

His words cut deeper than the physical pain. The tears I'd been holding back finally spilled over.

* * *

May 2017, Hawaii

Our wedding venue was a small, private estate on the North Shore of Oahu. My love for Paul should've been carrying me along, but the weight of my mother's accusations and the grief over my father's death was hardening my heart.

The beach unfurled into the mists beyond, and our local Hawaiian officiant started with a native chant, asking us to touch foreheads. He explained that the rain meant a spirit, or someone we loved, was present with us. I fought back tears, hoping that my father was there in spirit.

The wedding was bittersweet. Despite the rain, we enjoyed delicious food, and danced and laughed with our best friends. But underneath it all, a chill lingered, a reminder of the pain and uncertainty that surrounded us.

TOO MUCH

Paul's parents, though not entirely approving of our hasty marriage, showed their support. As the night wound down, my new father-in-law handed Paul an envelope full of cash. Paul snatched it from my hand, his voice harsh: "That's mine!"

His sudden aggression startled me. My pearl bracelet, a gift from Dad, snapped in the struggle, scattering pearls across the wet lawn. "This was from my dad! You asshole!" I cried, scrambling to gather the precious beads.

Paul stormed away. The rain fell harder, mirroring the storm raging within me. I chased after him, Mary, our loyal wedding planner, trailing behind, her concerned eyes searching mine.

"We need to find Paul," I said. The driver found him pacing on the side of the road. We sat in silence the entire way back to the cottage, listening to the rhythmic swish of the wipers bashing the windshield. Paul stumbled to bed, his movements sluggish and uncoordinated. Minutes later, he was passed out.

The darkness of the soothing ocean was calling me. I opened a bottle of wine and took the flowers with me to the lanai. Underneath the starless sky, pretended that our wedding night didn't end so miserably. Listened to the waves in pure solitude. Just me and the ebb and flow of crashing on the rocks. A steady rhythm and reminder of what could always be one constant in the chaos of my broken life.

That's when I let myself cry.

* * *

Roses

July 4, 2017, Oahu Beach Park, Hawaii

The sun beat down on the crowded beach, a symphony of sizzling hot dogs, sticky popsicle drips, and squealing children. Fourth of July in Hawaii. A chance to celebrate "America" and our induction into military surgical residency training. But the festive atmosphere couldn't cheer me up from what was happening between Paul and me. He was noticeably absent.

I spotted Dr. Thatcher, his brown tousled hair tucked underneath a Yankees cap. A bit of nervous anxiety rushed inside of me as I remembered our coffee talk and whatever delusional future I envisioned on my drive home that evening.

"Hi Cindy, where's Paul?" Dr. Bates startled me, blocking my view of Dr. Thatcher.

"He's... he's home," I lied. Paul signed up to drive for a rideshare company. It was driving him crazy to sit around at home all day thinking of new strategies to get out of his legal loophole.

"Oh," Dr. Bates replied, a hint of disappointment in his tone. He shifted his attention, introducing me to his family. His wife was stunning, her perfectly coifed curls a radiant contrast to my messy top-bun.

Later that evening, Paul's embrace felt more like a habit than a lifeline as I walked through the door. But a flicker of hope briefly ignited within me, a desperate longing for the connection we had in the beginning. I leaned into him, my fingers tracing the familiar contours of his back, my lips seeking his.

TOO MUCH

In the darkness of our bedroom, we undressed in silence, the routine replacing the passion we once shared. For a fleeting moment, the world outside faded away, replaced by the warmth of his skin against mine, the rhythm of our breaths mingling in the air.

As we lay entwined in the aftermath, a familiar emptiness settled between us, heavier than before. The conviction changed us. Changed what we had—and I feared things between us would never be the same.

CHAPTER 5

Notes

August 2017, Side's Hospital, Hawaii

The pager's shrill cry ripped through my thoughts—another reminder that I wasn't just Cindy, grieving daughter and worried wife. I was Dr. Neighbors, surgical resident, and I was needed. *Now.* My heart pounded as I sprinted back to the nurse's station, my heavy clogs sliding along the freshly mopped floors. Just two weeks into my rotation at Main Hospital's sister training hospital—Side's, I was already drowning.

It wasn't until I started writing that I realized some people assume doctors roll out of bed looking squeaky clean like we're straight from your screen, rounding on the same patients in the same hospital doing the same routine.

I know you don't want to hear me whine about it but, I was a loner. Each day was a desperate scramble to keep up—deciphering the hieroglyphics of the electronic medical records, triple-checking medication dosages, all while fielding texts about Paul's legal woes and dodging my mother's venomous emails. A juggling act fueled by sugary snacks and bitter coffee.

As I burst through the double doors of the nurse's station, the fluorescent lights seared my retinas. The familiar tightness threatening to erupt into full-blown panic. *Had I screwed something up? Forgotten a critical order?*

I scanned the faces of the nurses, their stoic expressions giving nothing away. Just another day in the life of a surgical resident, I thought bitterly, forcing a shaky smile onto my face. *Fake it till you make it, right?*

But deep down, I was crumbling. The weight of grief, exhaustion, and self-doubt threatened to crush me. The charge nurse jabbed a finger in my direction.

"Dr. Neighbors, where's the note for Mr. Tanaka's dressing change?" Her voice, sharp and accusatory, sliced through the sterile air.

My mind raced, frantically replaying the morning's events. Mr. Tanaka... dressing change... I had been in his room with my senior resident. We'd changed the dressing together, discussed his wound healing, but... had I documented it? A cold dread tightened in my stomach.

"Dr. Neighbors?" The charge nurse's voice dripped with impatience. "Do you even know what's going on here? Two months in, and you're still struggling with the basics. And where's your badge?"

Humiliation, hot and stinging. I mumbled an apology, the words catching in my throat. Before I could offer an explanation, she dismissed me with a curt wave, her eyes scanning the station for her next victim.

Later that afternoon, a call from Dr. Bates confirmed my worst fears.

Notes

Paul had lost his spot in the Urology program. The news landed like a sledgehammer to my chest, the air whooshing out of my lungs.

"Dr. Bates, please," I pleaded. "There must be something we can do. He's a good person..."

We went back and forth for a few minutes, but my pleas fell on deaf ears. Dr. Bates, though sympathetic, was firm. The decision was final. And I was being pulled from the rotation at Side's.

"Cindy, I want you to graduate from this residency program unscathed," he said. I resigned from a battle I wouldn't win and let those be the last words.

As much as I tried to reason with myself that he was right, this felt like punishment. The missed note, the nurse's station... not fitting the stereotype of a local doctor. It sounds crazy, but my theory was that I was "too white."

But back at Main Hospital, I wasn't fitting in either. Constantly asked what ethnicity I was—if I was Hawaiian since I claimed to be from Hawaii. I was sick of having to explain my skin color. What being "hapa" means—I wanted to say I was the same as everyone else. Human.

I texted Paul a selfie of me in my scrubs, smiling with my iced coffee. He'd never understand. He'd think it was my fault for not wearing a badge, for not writing a note, for snapping at a nurse. When the day ended, I snuck off to a burger food-truck, the savory smell of fried onions and garlic masking the sterile scent of the hospital stuck on

51

my scrubs—a moment of bliss. But shoveling the burger into my mouth didn't stop the tears from streaming down my face.

* * *

September 2017, Hawaii

Only three months into residency, I was a walking zombie. Each day becoming more of a scramble for survival, a never-ending game of whack-a-mole with medical crises. On sheer coffee and adrenaline, I navigated the maze of hospital hallways, the blur of pages, computer screens, and vending machine sustenance.

At home, Paul's fate hung in the balance. The Urology residency was unable to find an immediate replacement, which offered a sliver of hope, a lifeline for our white-knuckle desperation. But the uncertainty consumed us, always the undercurrent of our strained conversations. The joy we once found in each other's company had withered, replaced by resentment and unspoken blame.

Our apartment echoed with the hollow silence of a countdown to an unknown future. Every glance, every sigh, seemed to carry the weight of a million possibilities. And yet, I only wanted one—an impossibly perfect future gilded from our wreckage.

My professional life was starting to feel like a battleground. Dr. Bates sent an email. My notes were "weak." On another occasion, he pulled me aside, warning me about my "dismissive" attitude, because I had been texting during a lecture. His departure left me adrift, replaying in my mind: *"graduate unscathed."* After receiving the accusations from my mom, his words felt like child's play. *Weak? Dismissive?* Even if I felt weak, at least I could laugh about it.

With Paul's possible discharge looming, I cared more about his medical career than my own at this point. The more I cared about his future, the more our vows seemed like a cruel joke. It was a paradox I couldn't escape. The memory of Paul's anger, the shattered pearl bracelet—the entire spectacle haunted me. It was like Paul didn't appreciate me. Everything I had done for him.

Sometimes the hospital became my refuge, a demanding distraction from Paul's indifference. But the competitive environment, fueled by petty rivalries and power struggles, also proved to be just as callous. I faced sexism from all genders, navigating a system where female colleagues were also threats, rather than allies.

Dr. Bates informed me that he'd received anonymous complaints from nurses on various floors at Main. He showed me emails that he said were concerning. People said I was rude. Condescending. Short.

Despite the challenges, I pushed forward, determined to prove my worth. But the weight of it all—the stress, the uncertainty, the crumbling marriage—it was taking its toll. I felt my dreams slipping like sand through my fingers.

The question lingered: *Could I salvage Paul's career, the marriage, stay on track with my residency...or was I destined to crack?*

Teetering on edge, I kind of knew, but I kind of didn't.

* * *

TOO MUCH

October 2017, Main Hospital, Hawaii

Dr. Bates called me into his office. My shoulders tensed as I approached his door. His office was always in disarray, making it questionable if he ever spent much time at home. Various clothes scattered his floor, with piles of used scrubs shoved into the corner. Energy drinks and protein bars toppling out of the cabinets.

It was sweet that he had his family photos framed, cute triplets and his perfect wife—the quintessential American family. Except for his recent diet and obsession with energy drinks and protein bars.

"Dr. Neighbors," he said, not looking up from his desk. "Come in, please."

I stepped inside, my heart pounding. Was this about another complaint? Had I done something wrong? Before I could ask, a young, blonde woman in uniform brushed past me, her gaze fixated on me before she disappeared down the hall.

Dr. Bates cleared his throat. "Specialist Kinsley," he said, acknowledging her with a nod. Then he turned his attention back to me. "We need to talk about your communication style."

"Sir?" I asked, my voice tight. "Did someone complain?"

He leaned back in his chair, steepling his fingers. "It's not one incident, Dr. Neighbors. It's a pattern. Your tone, your demeanor... People find it abrasive."

"Abrasive?" I repeated, trying to keep my voice steady. "Can you give me an example?"

He hesitated, then said, "It's not so much what you say, it's how you say it. Your tone can come across as...rude."

"I'm not sure I understand, sir," I said. "Can you be more specific?"

He sighed, as if I were the one being difficult. "Dr. Neighbors, I'm trying to help you. We all have areas we need to work on. Maybe you could try softening your tone a bit, smiling more..."

I felt a surge of anger, but I kept my voice even. "I'm always professional, sir. I'm not sure what else I can do."

He leaned forward, his voice dropping to a conspiratorial whisper. "My wife tells me all the time that I have RBF—resting bitch face. It's something I actively monitor. I think we all have it to some degree, but some of us need to work on it...more than others."

I stared at him, unsure how to respond. Was he seriously comparing me to his wife? And suggesting that I had resting bitch face?

He seemed oblivious to my discomfort. "It's something to think about," he said, dismissing me with a wave of his hand.

I left his office feeling humiliated and angry. His words echoed in my mind, a constant reminder that my competence was secondary to my perceived likability.

* * *

TOO MUCH

October 2017, Downtown Honolulu, Hawaii

I desperately needed a girl's night out. Met up with Gabi and Jennifer—they were residents at Main, too. We all went to med school together. Gabi was Peds and Jennifer was OBGYN. We tried to meet up once a month for mimosas or boozy beach days. Gabi was the Gossip Queen at Main. Always dressed to the nines when we went clubbing, the kind of girl who could party all night, but still pre-round before everyone else. The kind of girl who said she never studied, but secretly did. Jennifer—she was an earthy, bohemian type, always meditating, gardening—lived on a farm with her parents on the island. Very chill and grounded. Wanted to come back and live on the island when she was done with the military. I don't blame her; there's no place like Hawaii.

The sweet aroma of lemongrass and chili filled the air as we squeezed into a cozy booth at Hawaiian Thai, a hidden gem tucked away in a bustling side street of downtown Honolulu. The walls were adorned with vibrant tapestries and twinkling fairy lights, creating an intimate and inviting atmosphere. As we sipped on our colorful cocktails, the latest hospital gossip flowed freely between us.

I longed to share the humiliating comment Dr. Bates made about my "resting bitch face." Instead, I listened as Gabi and Jennifer dissected their latest dating drama mixed with juicy intern mishaps, their voices a mix of amusement and indignation.

"Can you believe Ryan forgot to order a post-op scan?" Gabi exclaimed, her eyes wide with mock horror.

"And then he blamed it on the nurse!" Jennifer chimed in, shaking her head in disbelief.

I forced a laugh, the taste of bitterness lingering on my tongue. Their gossip felt trivial compared to the weight of my own burdens.

"So, how's Paul doing?" Jennifer asked, her voice softening as she reached across the table to squeeze my hand.

I hesitated, unsure how much to reveal. "He's... fine," I finally said. "Tell me about the new guy you're dating." They had no idea why Paul wasn't in residency—though they all suspected it. I always shut the conversations down. How could I possibly explain that my husband was convicted of a crime he didn't commit? And that I believed him, even if nobody else did? I didn't want to go down that rabbit hole...and worse, that we spent a mini-fortune defending the case, only to lose.

Gabi leaned in, her eyes sparkling with curiosity. "Any updates on Paul's residency situation?"

I shook my head, a familiar wave of anxiety cuing me to take another sip of alcohol. "Not yet," I mumbled.

Jennifer waved her phone at us both, "So—what do you think?" She flashed pics of a handsome brunette from her dating app. "He's kind of cute, right? I mean—we've gone out a couple times?"

"Yeah! Totally!" I was relieved. Jennifer was dating someone who seemed normal—that made one of us. And we could finally talk about something, other than drama.

TOO MUCH

* * *

November 2017, Main Hospital, Hawaii

Dr. Bates wasn't the only one who had opinions about my appearance. A few months into residency, I started wearing my white coat every day. Without it, I would invariably get interrogated, "Are *you* my nurse? When is the doctor coming? I've been waiting so long already."

"Oh, I'm the doctor."

"You? No. How old are you! You're too pretty!"

"Um…what brings you in today?"

"Are you married?"

Even though I'd make a point to flash my ring back, my gender made me fair game for objectification. Pretty privilege only took me so far with my patients. After trialing my white coat, and various ways of answering the question, or not answering it at all, I became numb to it. I guess I did develop "resting bitch face."

One morning, I was presenting morning rounds with two other interns. When I finished, Adam, the intimidating one, stared at me intently. He said, "If you looked at an attending like that, I swear to God, you would be told to leave. You would be kicked out in a heartbeat. Never make that face again."

What face? I'd been nervously looking for feedback, so his accusation made no sense. A rush of shame and embarrassment came over me. I thought I had simply been existing, doing my job.

I nodded. After evening rounds, I asked the other chief what happened.

"Well, you have an expressive face, so you need to be careful. I'm sure you didn't mean anything by it. But sometimes, I think you just give people the wrong look, and they can take it the wrong way. Don't worry about Adam, though," he said, as if that would make me feel better. "He was just in a bad mood."

But the advice made me feel worse. I wondered if Adam had ever been written up by leadership for his face or tone of voice. I couldn't appear unguarded, lest I risk being accused of being a bitch for speaking in a tone, or being rude. Adam's mood was okay. Warranted, even.

Not sure how my face was any different from what others would do... Steve slamming his phone down, cursing about nurses who needed an order. Tony trudging his clogs through the halls, muttering, "I'm always the black cloud." Dr. Bates, on his self-proclaimed intermittent fasting diet, sneaking malasadas from the resident lounge when he thought no one was looking.

Despite the extra heavy systemic gaze following me around, I did well on paper. My first program evaluations commended me for my medical knowledge and experience, which were consistent with expectations for a first-year.

By the middle of intern year, I had my first publication. By the middle of my second year, I won two first prize awards for research on reducing postoperative opioid use. I was doing everything expected of me. Or so I thought.

Nobody cared about my academic achievements. They only seemed to care about my "tone of voice," the "facial expressions," the "bitchy" air. Soon enough, the label stuck. I was the "bitchy" ENT resident at Main Hospital.

Was it my fault? Probably. I hated it there. I couldn't help but let it show. The endless hours, the constant pressure, the feeling of being trapped in a system that seemed designed to break me down.

I longed for an escape, a way out of this suffocating existence. But every time I thought about quitting, a voice said: *Keep going*. As the days turned into weeks and an entire year passed by, that voice grew fainter, its words drowned out by the relentless drone of self-doubt and despair. I was losing myself.

* * *

December 2018, Hawaii

As Paul applied for residency spots, I faced my bi-annual residency review, a dreaded event where attendings scrutinize residents' performance. Dr. Bates, the program director, presented a stack of negative peer evaluations, highlighting my "rude and condescending" behavior and lack of interpersonal skills. Despite acknowledging my strong medical knowledge, he placed me on remediation, a program designed to address my perceived deficits. The news was devastating, but a small compliment on my notes offered a glimmer of hope amidst the overwhelming negativity.

Notes

Later that week, I ran into Dr. Thatcher in the OR. We were just passing each other. Even in scrubs, there was an undeniable magnetic chemistry between us. He smiled and reached his hand out to give me a high five. I reached back and we high-fived each other. So awkward. Were we flirting? I don't know. I shuffled my legs, pretended to look at something interesting on the floor, like my work clogs. And then quickly checked around to see which nurses might be watching us. Thankfully none. We smiled at each other. He asked how I was doing. I wasn't going to admit I had just been placed on remediation, for being rude. I wanted him to think I was nice. Even though he was married. A small part of me hoped he was getting divorced—I knew it was wrong to think that way. But I couldn't help it. Maybe this is just who I am. We each went on with our day, but at least he made me smile and forget Dr. Bates, the drama with Paul, and my hopeless future—even if was for only for a few seconds.

CHAPTER 6

Degrees

January 2018, Main Hospital, Hawaii

Hope I'm not boring you with too much of this hospital stuff. I was 18 months deep into residency at this point, sitting with my "mentor," interrogation style. A single fluorescent bulb flickered overhead, casting harsh shadows on us both. I was older than Dr. Pratt, so I hated calling her "ma'am." I didn't want to admit that I looked up to her, but I did. A female Viking. Tall, brunette, green eyes. Bold voice. Like she dropped out of the sky and fell into this Army surgeon life. Reminded me of Paul—heroic—because she probably would have had it easier as a model, rather than fighting in the trenches of Main. Her walls were decorated with nothing but degrees from Ivy Leagues. Not a single plant in the dreary space. No ocean view.

"Cindy," Dr. Pratt began, her voice crisp and professional, "these mentorship meetings are designed to help you succeed." Her gaze settled on me, expectant.

I hesitated. "There's something I want to talk to you about..." I finally mumbled, my voice, barely audible, above the hum of her leaky mini-fridge in the corner of the stale room.

"Of course," Dr. Pratt leaned forward. "You can talk to me about anything here. This is a safe space." She flashed her perfectly white teeth at me. The words felt hollow, like she was reading lines from a script.

I took a deep breath and plunged in. "The residents...did you know they have a question bank for the in-service exam?"

Dr. Pratt's face hardened with disapproval. "I'm going to pretend you didn't just say that," she said, her voice cold.

It felt like my heart stopped. "What?"

She changed the subject and asked what cases I had that morning, how I felt about the case we did together earlier in the week...how I had been coping with the pressures of residency. If I had an outlet for stress. She asked about Paul and I lied.

"Paul and I are fine—he's trying to figure out his next plan. But we are good—just had a nice dinner and we try to take some time to ourselves..." my voice trailed off. I picked at my nails and looked at her plaques. Thought about asking if she was going to have kids anytime soon and reminded myself that would be inappropriate. But I was curious.

"Cindy," she continued, her tone shifting to one of feigned concern, "have you been seeing the therapist with the other residents? How is that going?"

I felt anger, followed by shame. I wanted to scream, to defend myself, but I lied again. "I don't know," I mumbled. "I mean—I think it starts next week."

Dr. Pratt's eyes softened. "Why don't you work on smoothing things out with the other residents? Everyone wants to help you get back on track with the program."

I nodded, my mind racing. Smooth things out? Was she serious? Did she not understand the gravity of what I just said? Was I insane? Just imagining things…?

As I left Dr. Pratt's office, a sense of dread washed over me. Her parting words echoed in my ears: "Stay positive." But how could I, when it felt like the walls were closing in around me? The empty, white hospital corridors stretched out before me, cold and impersonal, like my future unfolding.

* * *

February 2018, Main Hospital, Hawaii

"Cindy," his voice boomed, "what's the differential?"

The ENT conference room crackled with tension as Dr. Pang, fixed his stern gaze on me. Is it wrong that Dr. Pang could have been any man in that room? They were all the same to me at this point. Pang, Bates, Pratt, Attending. (Unless Dr. Thatcher was there, of course).

To the attendings, so were we. *"Resident."* Sometimes, I was accidentally called "Steve." Not joking. But today, they meant *Cindy.*

My heart hammered. Fumbling with the mouse, my mind a chaotic swirl of legal jargon and Paul's case, I scanned the radiology study

presented on the projector screen. Stammered out a few hesitant possibilities, whatever I could think of, "Uh, neck mass, cancer—"

"Papillary thyroid cancer. Metastatic cancer. Lymphoma," Steve, my
ever-confident co-resident, interjected. He had a gentle, reassuring
presence, his voice a calm amidst the storm of the conference room.
His notes were always meticulously organized, unlike the frantic
scribbles in my collection of notebooks.

Dr. Pang's praise for Steve sent a tide of humiliation through me. I
sank deeper into my chair, pretending to take notes in my journal
that was filled with my all my notes about Paul. Friday mornings were
brutal. Academic sessions turned into gladiatorial combat, attendings
circling the residents, eager to pounce on any misstep.

It was a game not to look at my phone as the morning droned on.
Differentials and mnemonics faded into a haze as thoughts of Paul
consumed me—the injustice, the pressure, the relentless fight for his
future. A burning resentment simmered within, directed not just at
the Army, but at the entire medical world that seemed to prioritize
ego over empathy.

Steve, on the other hand, was thriving. He memorized Pasha, the
ENT bible, cover to cover, while I poured my energy into the Army's
legal code, AR-600-20. I was consumed with the goal of freeing Paul
from the shackles of his wrongful conviction.

ENT residents are expected to expertly interpret scans despite zero
radiology training. Failure equates to public evisceration. It's trial by
fire. By graduation, we should be able to interpret head and neck
scans better than most radiologists—we were told.

I learned to temper my knowledge, playing dumb to avoid the wrath of bruised male egos. "Excuse me, sir, um, I was just wondering if there's something there?" was my go-to phrase, delivered in a carefully crafted "Barbie in the Army" voice.

That day, my lack of preparation caught up with me. Too absorbed in drafting a letter for Paul's lawyer to focus on the case. My chief let out an audible sigh as I fumbled through the scan. Like the star quarterback from the opposing team, Steve swooped in again, this time with a KITTENS mnemonic. His recitation flawless, his demeanor unwavering.

Dr. Pang beamed like Steve was his long-lost protégé child. Steve was the favorite.

Is it bad that I found Academics to be quite boring? God awful even. I couldn't help myself from caring more about Paul than these scans and surgical jargon.

I needed people in this program to help me. I needed allies—but all I had were frenemies.

* * *

February 2018, Main Hospital, Hawaii

Dr. Thatcher had this effortless charm. His infectious laugh and genuine warmth drew me in. It wasn't just his charm. Everyone gravitated towards him in the OR. He seemed to have this secret recipe for happiness, his presence radiating a soft, golden light. The guy worked hard, but he was humble about it.

Degrees

We bumped into each other in the cafeteria, and chatted over scrambled eggs and coffee. I confessed that I was considering another residency. He offered me some unexpected advice. Leaning in, his voice barely above a whisper, he said, "Keep your head down. You don't want to be *too* good at anything here, especially in the military. Stay in the middle of the road."

Isaac walked by and they waved hello.

"You don't think I should quit ENT?"

"No—you're a great surgeon. Don't quit." I really hoped he would have told me to quit. But I wasn't getting the answers I wanted, so I changed the subject. "What do you think of Isaac?"

"That's—I shouldn't be talking about other residents with you—" he smirked, like he was flirting.

"Oh—sorry," I blushed.

"Isaac is smart," he smiled at me. "I offered him the same advice. He had similar—issues a couple years ago. Every resident has issues, Cindy. You don't want to stand out."

I couldn't help but wonder if he was talking about me with my attendings. Was this a minefield of hidden agendas and power plays? I tried to shake off the unease, something didn't sit right with me. We parted ways and I continued to tell myself that it was normal for a junior resident to be grabbing coffee and breakfast with a surgical attending. Focused on my theories and his words. Isaac had issues?

Isaac was brilliant but insecure, constantly reminding us that he was a trust-fund baby, flexing his wealth and accomplishments, desperate for recognition. Yet, his true advantage lay in a secret cache—a 150-page Google doc filled with answers to the most frequently asked questions on the in-service exam.

His blatant cheating baffled me. He was a graduate of a top medical school, his intellect undeniable. Why risk it all? Maybe the pressure of residency had cracked even his seemingly impenetrable veneer. He shared his illicit cheat sheet with me during intern year, tempting me with a shortcut to success. I'd always been a good test-taker, but the in-service exam loomed over me like a dark cloud, its importance both inflated and minimized by those around me.

My growing disdain for residency killed my motivation to study, to stay in the residency program altogether. The conflicting messages left me feeling lost and uncertain. Was this the path I needed to take? Was compromising my integrity the price of survival in this hyper-competitive environment?

After all, when I tried to tell Dr. Pratt about it, she seemed to look the other way—almost as if she was encouraging me to use it. Maybe that's what I was supposed to do…*cheat? Is this what it would take to fit in?*

Then, a new *thing* was born—I rehashed all those nights Paul and I slaved away memorizing what I thought were useless facts until it mattered when my dad died—even if I was studying all that time to impress Paul in the beginning. *I hustled. Worked hard to get into AOA to get here—for this? Just so I could pretend to be "middle of the road" and play games for an answer bank…?*

Degrees

The more I obsessed about it all, the more it annoyed me...yes, I wanted the answer bank—part of it was FOMO, part of it was greed. A power play. Honestly, maybe a part of me wanted to cheat. I could be like Isaac. "Smart." I just knew that I didn't want to cheat or kiss people's asses for it. The spiraling thoughts made me sick.

* * *

March 2018, Hawaii

The mandatory "group" therapy felt like a joke. Dr. Bates, ever the pragmatist, had deemed it "too much" to have more than two residents in a session. So instead, I was subjected to a series of one-on-one meetings with each resident, a therapist awkwardly mediating the forced pleasantries.

Isaac and I met once with the therapist. It was stiff. We awkwardly smiled at each other and went through our history of how we first started working together—pretended everything was fine.

"I don't have any issues with Cindy," he said with a forced smile. He rubbed his wrist and checked his designer watch. I think he hated spending an hour of his day there. We all did, I guess. If we couldn't be honest in a therapy session, what were we even doing there?

"Um—yeah, I mean, I don't have issues with Isaac, either." Even if I did, it would have been wrong to say so. He was an upper resident. This whole thing felt utterly pointless. Embarrassing. Even worse, I conjured up the courage to text Isaac for the latest answer bank.

Isaac emailed it to me just in time for the upcoming exam. I really had to be careful around him. I didn't have a chance to review all the questions and answers, but it was legitimate. A cliff notes version of all my ENT textbooks I never had time to read. Even though I didn't want to be nice to Issac, I was obligated.

With the other residents, I could still feel tension. I guess it was my bitchy attitude. I didn't tell anyone else that I had the questions—except Steve. I didn't want it to blow up in my face, especially since it felt like Dr. Pratt didn't seem to mind. Therapy with the other residents felt like a choreographed dance, each interaction a rehearsed performance of professionalism and cooperation. Nothing changed, nothing was resolved. It was just Dr. Bates ticking off a box on his checklist. But having a cheat sheet, somehow inspired me. Like I could ace the test and get through this program if people could just "like me."

I decided to take matters into my own hands.

Tony, the jacked pro-football-wannabe-turned-resident, with his perfect model smile, hipster clothes, and a cute girlfriend perpetually on his arm, was particularly hostile towards me. Patients swooned over him, drawn to his carefully sculpted physique and practiced charm. He'd snap behind closed doors in the resident room, kicking his feet, slamming the phone down. Cursing just as much as I did. He was infamous for typos, which is why I sensed he wrote heinous comments about me—riddled with poor spelling and grammatical errors.

Beneath the bravado, I sensed a kindred spirit, someone just as hungry for validation as I was. One evening, I reached out to him, hoping for a truce. We met the next day at an outdoor mall in Hawaii Kai, the sun glaring as we sought refuge in the shade.

Degrees

"So, you wanted to meet?" Tony asked, sipping his iced matcha.

"Yeah," I began, hating the uncertainty in my voice, but channeling my inner "Barbie in the Army" persona nonetheless. "It's about the peer evaluations. I'd love to talk through any issues and find a way to work better together."

Tony scoffed, a dismissive wave of his hand. "Cindy, there's no 'together' here. *You're* the problem. You're the reason we're stuck in this therapy charade."

He paused, his voice lowering slightly. "Look, I've been through some rough patches myself. I had to take a long, hard look in the mirror and make radical changes. Sometimes, that's what it takes. Radical change."

His words stung. A burning anger flared within me. Radical change? Why couldn't anyone else change, even a little?

Tony scrolled through his phone, tapping away, and then "Hey— sorry, I gotta go—something came up with Lia, but—we should do this again sometime, yeah? Could surf bowls with us?" He offered a smile and I couldn't help but smile back, like everything was fine, even though it seemed like we got nowhere. He knew I wasn't good at surfing— it was a passive-aggressive jab to invite me surfing in town.

When I returned home, Paul informed me of the news we were hoping wouldn't come true. He was getting discharged from the Army because of the conviction. The silver lining was that he could apply for civilian residency while waiting to be discharged.

"Maybe I just won't practice medicine," he said.

"Are you kidding me? And do what? Drive tourists around?" I was exasperated. I couldn't believe he was about to give up after everything we did to fight the conviction.

"I dedicated my whole life to serving in the Army. Joined when I was 18. What am I supposed to do now?"

"Apply for residencies, Paul! Hello?" I was rude, mean. Yelling at him like how I yelled at my dad in the car on those drives home. I could have been kinder, but I couldn't help myself. I was mad. Mad at the Army. Mad at Main Hospital. Mad at the world. Paul lost his career. Most of all, I was mad at myself. I couldn't help but feel guilty. This was my fault and I had to fix it.

"Paul," I lowered my voice. "Apply anywhere. Honestly, if you want to do Urology on the mainland, we can figure it out. I want you to do whatever you want. But don't quit medicine. You can apply anywhere." I kissed him and reassured him. In my mind, I was reassuring myself. I needed Paul to be okay.

The big annual in-service exam was looming around the corner, and as I studied for the first time, the thought of Paul and I not being together hit me. What if he matched into a program on the mainland? Would our marriage survive? What if we...broke up?

The week following, the exam was a total disaster. I heeded Dr. Thatcher's advice and aimed for average, resisting the temptation to use Isaac's cheat sheet. But the questions were far harder than I anticipated, many of the terms unrecognizable. To be honest, I barely had time to study. I barely had time to care.

During the break, the residents gathered in the lounge, openly discussing the questions and answers. One of the residents bragged about having recorded dozens of questions and answers on their phone, promising to add them to Isaac's document. A sense of camaraderie filled the room as we swapped answers, but a nagging guilt settled in the pit of my stomach.

During the second half of the exam, seeing many of the exact questions we just discussed felt like a cruel joke…was I supposed to pick the answer choices my co-residents said they picked? The ones we just looked up together? What if we were wrong and got caught? Should I just guess instead?

The answer choices kept rotating in my head—if it wasn't clearly correct, my mind was playing tricks…this or that…true or false…A or B or C or D. A or B. No. C. D. A or B. Or C.

I didn't know what the right answer was. Later that night, I couldn't sleep. Felt guilty for having access to the answers. But—also felt guilty for *not* studying the Google doc. Curious how many I missed, logged in to finally review the masterpiece.

Unbelievable. New questions already added. Part of me felt stupid for not participating. Now I was sure to bomb the exam. It was graded on a curve. Paul possibly moving off island. I was sinking deeper into a bottomless pit of failure. I felt ashamed. Couldn't I have taken an hour or two to memorize these stupid test questions and answers?

And then the worst thought came at me...what if I didn't study or cheat because I didn't actually care? *No.* I was just distracted. I cared. I just couldn't focus.

I told Paul about the Google doc the next morning while we got ready for work. How I failed. How I failed to memorize the answers. I was expecting him to be outraged that I didn't study like the others... But his reaction surprised me. "Report it," he urged, his eyes gleaming with a vengeful fire.

I hesitated. *Report it?* I should have just done what everyone else did so at least one of us could succeed. Reporting it felt like betrayal, yet staying silent felt like complicity. I was trapped in a moral maze, unsure of the right path forward.

A few days later, I bumped into Dr. Pratt in the bustling hospital hallway. Her hair was pulled back in a tight ponytail, her face etched with a familiar mask of cool professionalism.

"Cindy," she greeted me with a curt nod. "How are things?"

I fumbled with my ID badge, my mind flashing back to our conversation in her office. "Okay, I guess," I replied.

A knowing glint appeared in her eyes. Maybe someone reported the question bank. Maybe she knew I had it in my possession. Maybe Isaac saw that I opened the Google doc. I think people can see who opens them...maybe?

I suddenly pretended not to know about the conversation we had in her office...just like she wanted. It was only a matter of time until I'd be declared a cheater—and I hadn't even had time to study it—honestly…I was starting to lose interest in this entire situation. "Have you seen that movie yet?" she asked, her voice barely audible above the din of the hallway.

I shook my head, confused. "What movie?"

"Swimming with Sharks," she said, a sly smile playing on her lips. "Kevin Spacey. You should check it out. It might be…enlightening."

She patted my arm, her touch cold and impersonal, and then disappeared into the crowd. A shiver ran down my spine. Was I so forgetful that I didn't even remember talking to her about a movie? It left me with an unsettling feeling, like I was a pawn in a game I didn't understand.

* * *

May 2018, Hawaii

The relentless pace of residency felt like a never-ending audition, a constant battle to prove my worth. It was a chilling echo of my past life in Los Angeles, where casting directors sized me up with a single glance, slashing my dreams before I could utter a word. Too fat, not old enough, too young, too ethnic, not Asian enough.

My manager at the time encouraged me to adopt a Hispanic stage name, so I became "Cindy dela Cruz." For a handful of years, I barely scraped by to have a chance at minor roles, literally starving myself for attention. My manager, Tess, constantly compared me to more successful actresses, triple threats who could sing, dance, and act circles around me. It felt like I would never be enough in that world, so why even try? It was too cutthroat for me—it seemed. I'll never forget the day she dropped me. I missed an audition because I had to babysit for rent—I was devastated. Tess went on to manage one of the biggest stars, so I guess I don't feel so bad—one of us succeeded.

Compared to the entertainment industry, medicine seemed like a noble pursuit driven by service and compassion. I yearned for the American Dream and a chance to make a real difference in people's lives. But I soon discovered that medicine was just as riddled with pettiness and superficial judgments as "Hollywood." Surgeons strutting around like wannabe-gods with inflated egos. The hospital itself a battleground.

Worse, I found myself falling into the same superficial patterns I tried to escape. Despite the MD after my name, the husband I'd fought tooth and nail for, and the competitive residency program, I still felt like a desperate actress trying to pass as a doctor. Even my marriage, which I desperately tried to salvage, was collapsing beneath the weight of Paul's resentment and my own growing disillusionment. The taste of bile rose in my throat, a familiar tang from childhood dinners where my mother's thinly veiled criticisms were served alongside the rice. *You'll never be good enough.*

Through the rumor mill we learned that Paul's replacement in the Urology program was a brilliant woman. I was happy for her, a shimmer of hope in a field dominated by men. But Paul saw it differently.

"She only got the spot because she's a female... minority," he grumbled, his voice dripping with bitterness. "The system is rigged against guys like me now."

Degrees

His words twisted in my gut. Had I benefited from affirmative action? Or was his resentment a symptom of something deeper, a festering wound that refused to heal?

Over the past few months, our arguments about the unknown intensified, with our misplaced anger and paranoia seeping into every corner of our lives.

"Are you serious?" I retorted, my voice rising in disbelief.

"Oh, please," he scoffed

I couldn't hold back any longer. "You're part of the problem, Paul! You're not in jail right now because you're white. Privileged. How do you not see that?!"

"You're just as white and privileged, too."

The room crackled with tension. Our once shared dreams of a bright future now seemed like distant memories, replaced by a bitter reality that threatened to consume us both. The fight escalated, fueled by years of pent-up frustration and resentment. Seconds passed and we were locked in a physical struggle, our bodies colliding in a whirlwind of rage and despair.

I lunged at the bookshelf, tearing it from the wall in a fit of fury. Photos and frames crashed to the floor, glass shattering like my hopes. Paul stumbled back, his eyes wide with a mix of shock and fear. But the momentary satisfaction of defiance quickly gave way to terror. Paul lunged at me, his hands gripping my arms, his face contorted with rage. He slammed me to the floor, his weight pressing down on my chest.

I screamed. He clamped his hand tightly over my mouth, muffling my cries. My head throbbed against the carpet, the taste of dust filling my mouth.

"Shut up!" Paul hissed.

A sharp rapping on the door cut through the chaos. "Police! Open up!" a voice bellowed from the other side.

Paul froze, his grip loosening slightly. I gasped for air, my body trembling.

"Mr. Jackson?" the voice called again. "Is everything alright in there?"

Paul glanced at me, his eyes pleading for me to stay silent. I met his gaze, a mixture of fear and defiance swirling within me.

Should I scream? Should I tell them the truth? Or am I trapped…is this what happened to his ex? All those lies he said she told…were they true?

I closed my eyes, the weight of our shared deception crushing me.

"We're fine," Paul called out, his voice strained. "Just a marital disagreement."

The knocking stopped, replaced by the sound of retreating footsteps. Silence descended upon the room, heavy and suffocating. Paul

washed his hands in the kitchen sink. He went to sleep in the office—
cold, distant.

As if nothing happened. But he was wrong.

CHAPTER 7

Rules

December 24, 2019, Hawaii

Holidays don't matter in medicine. Paul was working, our marriage in shambles. I was stuck with Tony, the perpetual black cloud, on Christmas Eve. A twisted form of Stockholm Syndrome offered an eerie comfort—the familiar chaos of a hospital filled with suffering was a refuge compared to my own life. My condo, a hollow shell. Lynn's unfinished house, thick with the haze of Kyle's weed and the simulated gunshots and explosions of his video games, a recipe for my own unraveling.

"Do you have any plans this weekend?" he started, interrupting my note-taking and spicy tuna lunch.

"Not really—I mean, Paul is working—he's on ICU for Christmas. How about you?"

"Yeah, Lia and I are gonna try to go on a hike. Do Koko Head tomorrow. You're welcome to join if you want."

"Oh, thanks. I'm on call, so—"

His sudden interest in my plans seemed out of character, almost sus...

or maybe he was making a genuine effort to be a good colleague, a friend...Maybe he had ulterior motives. *Or he was just lonely. Like me.*

"Dude—did you hear what Dr. Bates said to one of the nurses in the OR?"

I looked up, intrigued. "What?"

"If we were in the Hunger Games," Tony hesitated, his eyes darting away, "who would win...?"

"No way! Who did he say?"

"Will or Steve," he mumbled, avoiding eye contact.

I knew he was holding something back. "And who'd die first?"

His silence was deafening. It felt like a spotlight shining directly on me. "Why weren't any residents scrubbed in?" I changed tactics.

"Clinic duty," he retorted. "Other attendings had 'admin days' or some crap."

I chuckled dryly, attempting to cut layers of lies, thick between us. But Tony's words kept on looping around: *"We're all in therapy because of you."*

As pretty as he was, the sting of his words lingered. *Therapy. Something Tony would never admit he secretly enjoyed. Especially if it was because of me.*

TOO MUCH

* * *

January 2020, Hawaii

After rushing out of Nurse Olivia's baby shower, I was five minutes late for my 1:00 PM patient. The techs were mesmerized with their phones, so I called my patient and roomed her.

Inside the exam room, chaos. Nothing prepped. I frantically searched for instruments, trying to recall the patient's history while making small talk. *Act normal,* I reminded myself, with my masked smile. I started to remove the bloody splints from her nose. Her initial disgust turned to relief. I reached for an ice pack. A knock interrupted us.

Dr. Pratt. She led me to her office. Her eyes narrowed. "Cindy," she began, "I have to formally counsel you. You slammed the door."

My stomach dropped. "There must be some misunderstanding," I protested. "The techs weren't doing their job..."

"It doesn't matter," she cut me off. "You can't slam doors and yell. I need you to write a memo about this."

I tried to replay the last few minutes of what happened. I started panicking, wondering if I removed just one or two bloody splints. "Can I please finish with my patient?" I asked, trying not to crack.

"Yes, of course. But please, be mindful of your behavior."

I nodded numbly, returning to the exam room. Forcing a smile at the techs. *Who said I slammed a door and why...? How could they? As they scroll on their devices.*

* * *

February 2020, French Polynesia

Paul and I were lucky to escape for a week-long getaway in Tahiti, shortly after the door-slamming allegation. But it was no exotic vacation. I weighed the most I had in my entire life.

Half-way into residency, I'd developed bad lifestyle habits without a consistent schedule. Constantly downing donuts, cookies, chocolates, and sugar-mocha blended coffees during my breaks didn't help. In surgery we are taught to sleep when you can, sh*t when you can, and eat when you can. Not in the healthiest fashion. Slipped back into binge drinking on the weekends. Didn't exercise and barely slept. My cortisol levels sky rocketed. I hated that this had become my life, but I convinced myself it was the only way to survive.

I felt anything but sexy. Paul and I stopped having sex. It had been at least a year. The New Year's before that we'd brought a stripper home from a club on a Mexican vacation—even that desperate move failed to salvage the marriage. I was so desperate, so drunk, so delusional. But it was no steamy event. The three of us barely made out before she took off with some cash.

In a way, I felt sorrier for myself that night than I did for the stripper. She was probably making just as much, if not more money than I was, and at least, enjoying herself? It was a twisted way to view the world. At least men were honest with her about what they wanted, that when they sexualized her body and made advances, she was getting paid for it—there was nothing covert or corrupt—it was Mexico, sure. But what I'm getting at, I guess, is that…it was honest. Does that make it wrong?

By this point, I was sure that Paul was sleeping with someone else. There was no other way to explain us living together without him initiating sex. My mind and soul were heavy with looming thoughts of having to face Dr. Bates when I got back to work. The only things that could make me happy at this point were the beautiful healing waves. Bottomless cocktails.

Sitting on our bungalow deck looking out at the clear blue-green water, I watched honeymooners wading in the ocean, walking up the dock, some with children and some without. I found myself wondering what were their lives like? Could I be them? I'd even take their screaming children if they wanted to trade for my husband, coworkers, and…job.

Even though we got a picturesque and perfectly romantic suite, I couldn't help but look out at the crashing waves in the distance and imagine our marriage tumbling out of control.

The next day, we went on a scuba drift dive with other advanced divers to find dolphins. The current was rough, and we were kicking against the surging water, trying to chase dolphins and take photos. My air was running low, and the divemaster seemed oblivious. A huge swell hit us, and I panicked. My camera housing smashed against the reef, and I clung to it, my nails digging into the coral.

Rules

Staring at my oxygen gauge, I realized I was running out of air. I had to surface. I inflated my red tube and floated to safety.

Back on the boat, I was furious. "I told you I was low on air!" I yelled at the divemaster. It wasn't his fault, really, but I was tired of fighting against everything. I was tired of holding on. This incident highlighted the bigger issue: I was quick to blame others, my anger simmering beneath the surface. I wanted to let go of everything, like I had let go of the coral underwater.

Maybe the answer wasn't to fight, but to accept, to surrender. When I came back from the trip, I drafted a resignation letter and saved it on my computer. But I didn't share it. Instead, I held onto the key to my own prison, still clinging to the hope that I could change things from the inside.

* * *

March 2020, Main Hospital, Hawaii

Dr. Pratt pulled me into the conference room, where Dr. Bates was perched on a Herman Miller chair. She sat on an older floral fabric rolling chair. They offered me a seat in the wooden stool across from them.

"Cindy," Dr. Pratt said.

"Yes, ma'am."

She nodded. "I briefed Dr. Bates on the incident before you took leave."

"Cindy, I apologize we are just sitting down now to talk about this," he told me. "I was working at Side's that day."

"Okay, sir," I said.

"Slamming a door in the clinic, especially in front of a patient, is unacceptable. It's unprofessional, not to mention unbecoming of an officer. Just think about what that says about us, our clinic, our hospital, and the Army."

"I didn't slam the door, though," I mumbled, but I could already feel myself giving up this fight. Sure, I had a resignation letter drafted. I daydreamed about letting go and floating away, but not like this. Not for doing my job.

He handed me several papers. "Cindy, we have statements from multiple people. It's what you said before you slammed the door."

"I don't understand. I told the techs I would get my own patient. I said, 'I got it.'"

"They said it was your tone, Cindy. It was condescending and short. We've talked about tone many times," he said.

"Yes, sir."

"That was the point of remediation. I thought we had made progress, but clearly it's still a major problem."

Dr. Pratt sat there, observing. I wished I could ask her what she *really* thought, but she was on their side.

Rules

"I didn't want to disturb your leave or holidays," he continued, "but just before you left, the CCC voted to place you on hospital-level probation. It's sixty days long. The requirements are listed in the packet. Starting today, you can't see clinic. You can't operate in the OR without an attending present, and you can't back up junior residents. At the end of the probation, we will reassess."

All I could do was stare at the view of the ocean behind Dr. Bates, a babbling bobble-head.

"Cindy, we really want you to become the best ENT that you can be," he said.

I continued staring at the ocean and didn't know what to say.

"Cindy, this is serious. If you don't pass, the next possibility could potentially be a vote for dismissal from the program."

There it was. I would spend five years training and not actually graduate. I tried aiming for the middle of the road. My test scores suffered. Nothing was good enough. I cleared my throat and looked for my condo in the distance.

All of my hopes and dreams, marriage and future…drifting away.

I barely had a husband. I barely had a family. Now I was losing my career, too. I was thirty-five years old. My classmates from high school were already attendings at civilian hospitals. Here, I had to call attendings my age or younger than me "sir" and "ma'am" and watch them climb up the chain of command.

It hit me with sudden clarity that all of this focus on my face and tone meant I had taken my eyes off the prize: graduation.

"Before I sign this, I want us to sit down with Dr. Kent." He was the Urology Program Director turned Graduate Medical Director. We'd known each other ever since he'd accepted Paul into his program.

"Absolutely, Cindy. I think that makes a lot of sense. Let's see how soon we can do that, and I'll let you know."

As I walked away, I flipped through the stack of papers he handed me to find two separate memorandums, one written by the enlisted sergeant of our clinic, Sergeant Ferguson, and another by the nurse who I'd said "I got it" to on the day in question. The statements were nearly identical. Only the signature blocks were different.

I found Sergeant Ferguson and asked if we could talk. In his office, I showed him the copied memorandums. He admitted to helping Specialist Pierce write her statement and apologized for the misunderstanding. Sergeant Ferguson suggested I might need help with my "on edge" behavior.

Later, Sergeant Ferguson got the door fixed and wrote a new memorandum stating he was "mistaken about me slamming the door, as he later inspected it and found it to be malfunctioning and placed a work order."

I couldn't wait to clear my name with Dr. Bates and the CCC. Unfortunately, when presented with this new memorandum and work order, Dr. Bates insisted that the probation was about my tone when I said, "I got it."

Rules

He surprised me with comments from my co-residents in a special round of 360-degree evaluations. He summarized them, citing that I was "too difficult, disrespectful, demeaning, overwhelmed during stressful times…"

The reasons went on and on, all about my interactions with others. He provided me with pages of comments. It was too much for me to read—so I buried them in a stack of other papers on my desk.

It was hard not to think that this was a conspiracy.

* * *

March 2020, Hawaii

Covid struck the world and nothing would ever be the same. We were mandated to stay at home if we weren't on call. All of our clinics and elective cases were canceled.

Paul was assigned to the ICU that month and when he wasn't working, he would sleep in the office. Neither of us could afford to get Covid. It would strain our respective residency programs.

I was grateful my father died when he did. If he'd been sick during the pandemic, I wouldn't have been able to handle being separated from him and dealing with the drama of Lynn.

When I was in the hospital, all of the scenes playing added to the stressful and desperate atmosphere of the medical environment during a terrifying pandemic. Nurses in full PPE held up iPads to unconscious patients so that loved ones could say goodbye.

TOO MUCH

We lived in a surreal dystopian movie. But there was no pause button. And no way of knowing if it would ever come to an end.

* * *

April 2020, Main Hospital, Hawaii

I hadn't seen Gabi or Jennifer in a few months—they were both rotating at outside hospitals before Covid shut everything down. We met for lunch at the hospital cafeteria.

"So what's the latest?" Gabi squealed. I was desperate for someone outside of my department to review the facts of my situation and offer a different perspective.

"Oh my gosh, Cin—did you get your nails done! How can you operate like that?" Jennifer asked, taking a bite of her salad.

"Oh, well—nobody really notices—" I reached for my sushi.

"That's disgusting," Gabi interrupted. "Just kidding. I love them. Pink!" She smiled. She was always funnier than me.

I couldn't bear to tell them I was about to be placed on probation status—one step away from getting booted from the program. Halfway through the residency. It was embarrassing. I was so desperate to confide in them, but I just couldn't confess my misfortune.

Gabi and Jen were lucky, it seemed. How did they not have these problems with their programs? Was it because they were in Peds and

Rules

OBGYN? Maybe it was easier for them to get along with their colleagues because those specialties welcomed females.

Or maybe the problem was me.

* * *

April 2020, Main Hospital, Hawaii

The three of us—Dr. Bates, Dr. Kent, and me—sat down to discuss the probation.

"Dr. Bates told me I have resting bitch face, and I really think it's inappropriate for me to be punished so harshly over the years because of my tone of voice and facial expressions." The words came out like vomit. I couldn't help myself.

Silence descended for a beat. A dark look passed over Dr. Bates's face, like I had told an inappropriate secret.

"Cindy," Dr. Bates said with a smile, "I didn't say *you* have resting bitch face." Then he turned to Dr. Kent and put on the charm. "I actually explained *to her*," he said smugly, "that my wife always tells *me* that *I* have whatever you call it…bitchy resting face?" He laughed as if this was all one big misunderstanding. "And that *I* need to work on it. Not that Cindy has it."

I was reeling. Not my boss gaslighting me about saying I had RBF. Right in front of Dr. Kent.

Dr. Bates acknowledged me again, "I'm so sorry if that's how you interpreted my story, Cindy. That wasn't my intention at all. I would never say that to a resident, subordinate, or colleague. Or anyone, for that matter."

There it was, the official story to forever replace what actually happened. Worse, he made it seem like my interpretation was the problem.

Dr. Kent looked at both of us and cleared his throat, as if to cut the tension. "Cindy, um, I'm really sorry you are going through all of this. It sounds like this was a misunderstanding, as Dr. Bates said. I don't think he would say that to you, so rest assured, nobody here is saying that about you. That is not the reason for the probation. We're responding to numerous comments from your colleagues and co-residents, as you can see." He gestured to the stack of fresh 360-degree evaluations.

"We can get you help. I have some therapists who see other doctors here in the hospital," Dr. Kent offered. "They're wonderful. Off the record, if I needed to see someone, I would see Dr. Owens. I can arrange everything for you."

I felt the overwhelming pressure to agree, to shut my mouth, and to accept probation.

"I feel trapped," I said, tears spilling down my cheeks.

There was nothing I hated more than silent, hot tears. Especially in front of two men who could easily decide that I was unprofessional or unstable or unreliable or unfit for residency.

They looked at one another and smiled, as if this was some kind of breakthrough. Instead, it felt like a complete breakdown. Of communication. Of trust. Of my will. Of me.

What if the truth was much worse? What if I really was trapped? And my whole life was a sick, slick lie? What if I was just pretending? For the sake of Paul. For the sake of my mom. For the sake of my reputation. Just to keep up. Just to keep going. What if the truth was that it was driving me insane?

What if they genuinely wanted to help? Maybe they wanted to set me free.

No. I refused to believe that.

I wanted this life. And I'd to do anything to fight for it.

CHAPTER 8

Rumors

April 2020, Main Hospital, Hawaii

I approached my meeting with Dr. Owens with skepticism. Especially because this was all arranged by my program, but I was out of options.

Dr. Owens, a full bird colonel in her Army uniform, exuded experience. Her warm smile and the subtle mirroring of my posture put me at ease. The offer of water, snacks, and chocolate was unexpected, I couldn't resist. It felt strangely comforting to be vulnerable.

"Thank you for squeezing me into your busy schedule," I said, savoring a chocolate peanut butter cup.

"No problem at all," she replied.

"You're the psychiatry program director, right?" I asked, unsure if the setting was intentionally designed to create a power imbalance, despite Dr. Kent's reassurances.

"Yes, but I'm nearing my five-year mark and might pass the position along," she said.

"How long have you been a psychiatrist?"

"Twenty-five years."

I suspected she knew about me through Dr. Bates. "You don't feel like hurting others either, do you?" she asked, referencing the comments in my file.

"No, ma'am. Honestly, I just feel overwhelmed and stressed," I admitted.

"I'm having issues with the program," I began, "but not the ones I'm accused of."

"Oh?"

"There's—it's been isolating. I have no one to talk to," I looked away. Embarrassed that I was seeing a psychiatrist in the middle of the work day.

Dr. Owens nodded.

"Now I feel like they're conspiring—making a paper trail against me. I don't know what to do. I've considered quitting.

"You just asked if I wanted to hurt others," I said, my voice trembling. "There must be awful rumors about me. The truth is, if I were to hurt anyone, it would be myself. And I feel the program would be happy if I did."

"I understand what you're saying," Dr. Owens finally responded. "Surgery is a difficult field for women. I have many female surgeon friends and patients."

I shifted in my seat.

May I share a story about a surgeon I met when I was an interviewing medical student?" she asked.

"Sure."

"There was this female surgeon who was seen as tough outside the OR, but her all-female team adored her. I was terrified to meet her. One day, a tech arrived late, apologizing profusely. She couldn't take the bridge because she was scared. The surgeon, without looking up, calmly asked why. The tech explained her fear, tearfully.

"The surgeon looked up, and the room fell silent. She said, 'Next time you drive here, don't be scared. Take that fucking bridge. Never take the long way again. Do you understand?'

"The tech nodded and scrubbed in. It was a good day in the OR. I realized this surgeon deeply cared for her team, but I also saw why she could be perceived as harsh."

I looked around Dr. Owens' office, at the thriving plants. I wanted to be like that surgeon, powerful and protective, but feared I'd never get the chance.

"You've made it far as a woman in military medicine," I said. "What advice can you offer? I'm told to smile more, change my tone, be nice. Is being fake the answer? Some women are naturally nice, but I'm not. How I'm talking now, this is me. People find me rude."

"I don't think you sound rude." Her words sounded encouraging, but I remained cautious.

"I feel like they want me to be someone I'm not. Isn't that a double standard? Men don't have to change themselves."

"Sometimes, we have to play the part," Dr. Owens explained. "Like with patients, we adopt a persona. If we know it's a game, we play by the rules to get ahead. It may be difficult at first, but it can become fun." She smirked, as if sharing a secret. But how could this ever be fun?

"I think it gets easier with time," she added. I sat in silence, reflecting on Sergeant Ferguson's concerns and Dr. Owens' story. "Maybe it's time I try medication," I finally said.

"Have you taken anything before?" she asked.

I hesitated, afraid of the information being used against me. "You won't share this with anyone, right?"

"Everything we discuss here is confidential."

I reflected. The idea of medication, once a distant possibility, now felt like a lifeline. Maybe it wasn't about being fake or playing a game. Maybe it was about finding a way to function, to survive, to reclaim some semblance of control over my spiraling thoughts and emotions.

"Well, then, I've tried multiple things," I admitted, the words tumbling out in a rush. "But nothing seems to stick. I just... I can't keep going like this."

Dr. Owens nodded, her eyes filled with understanding. "What has worked in the past? Any side effects? We can try to work around them."

"Wellspring helped with my anxiety and depression," I confessed, knowing there was more to the story. The mood swings, the racing thoughts, the dark depths of despair—I'd experienced it all. But I was desperate for relief, for a chance to quiet the storm raging within me.

"We can start there," Dr. Owens said, a reassuring smile on her face. "It's a good first step. And remember, this is a journey, not a destination. We'll find what works for you, together."

We continued talking. I told her about Paul, how my residency started off with my family breaking apart from my father passing away. And the hour was up. As I left her office, a flicker of hope ignited within me. Maybe medication wasn't a sign of weakness or failure. Maybe it was a tool, a way to reclaim my life and find a path towards healing. It was a gamble, but at this point, I was willing to try anything.

If the Wellspring didn't work, at least I had someone I could talk to.

* * *

April 2020, Hawaii

The following Monday, I still hadn't signed the probation proposal. Over the weekend, I took a deep dive into the allegations, cross-referencing them with my planner, with frustrating results. Some of the dates when I was apparently late to rounds, I wasn't even at Main Hospital. The reports in the evaluations were overblown or outright false.

Rumors

Rumors. Statements designed to shame me to the point that I would sign on the dotted line and accept punishment.

> She uses harsher tones and words when unnecessary...she has rudely spoken...slammed clinic doors out of frustration.

I went to the evaluation website to try and decode the comments further. There were more nasty ones than kind ones.

Dr. Bates was prioritizing the negative and ignoring the positive, which only made me want to fight back harder.

I spent my entire life believing that if I could just say the right thing or do the right thing, my mom would finally grant me her love and approval. Now I was in this the same toxic cycle with my unhinged co-residents and attendings. I knew they'd most likely made their minds up about me, but I was still looking for the secret combination of voice and tone and body language that might make it okay.

I spent the weekend compiling my own evidence and reconstructing a timeline to prove that some of these points were invalid or impossible. Nobody else had my best interests at heart. I couldn't stop fighting. I needed to show up for myself, even if nobody else would.

I started calling around to lawyers and documenting everything. I argued that this entire situation was a personal attack, a "he said-she said" type of situation.

A few days later, I was in an empty hallway, and Dr. Bates, dressed in his camo uniform, approached me from the other direction.

"Cindy—"

I tried to sidestep him and keep my eyes down, but he stepped in front of me, stopping me in my tracks. It seemed strange and threatening. He towered over me. It felt sinister.

"Cindy, I need that signed document," he said.

I didn't know how to tell him that I wasn't going to sign it. I didn't know how to say that I'd spent the better part of that week meeting with several attorneys. I didn't know how to tell him that I was going to fight him and this whole thing because it was bullshit.

"Dr. Bates, excuse me," I said.

He didn't move. "Cindy, you need to sign it now."

"Dr. Bates, I don't have my copy on me. And, honestly, I need my attorney to review it."

I hadn't retained an attorney yet, but I needed to buy myself some time and get him off my back. After a tense standoff, he stepped aside, and I pivoted, swallowing my tears, my throat tight. I walked back to the resident room, shaken. Adam was coming out, and, together, we walked toward the elevator for rounds. Dr. Bates rounded a corner, yelling, "Wait up, I'm coming."

I didn't know what to do, and I panicked. The last thing I wanted was to be around Dr. Bates again, so I pulled Adam aside. "I'll meet you up there. I forgot something."

Rumors

Dr. Bates had no choice but to get into the elevator alone, because I'm sure he didn't want to make a scene.

"What was that about?" Adam asked, sounding annoyed. He was the chief resident and supposed to be leading rounds, but I needed his support.

"Adam," I sobbed, finally breaking down, "I can't do this. I can't be here right now. I'm sorry, I can't round. I can't...I need to go, okay? I'm sorry. I'll explain everything to you later. Just tell Dr. Bates I had to go. I'm so sorry."

Standing there, having to explain myself, I realized that I'd been clinging to the hope that the program would come to its senses and rescind the probation. But clearly, that wasn't going to happen. I ran to the resident room and grabbed my belongings, my computer, and my ID badge, wiping my tears while I rushed down the stairwell to the family medicine clinic.

Thankfully, there were no patients in the waiting room. Two nurses were setting up the front desk station. I started crying again as I approached them. One lady looked concerned and confused, probably because I was wearing my scrubs and hospital badge.

"I need to see someone right now," I told them.

Even though they didn't know the situation, they could obviously see that I was upset. "Okay, okay, I'm just logging in. I just need a minute. Can I see your ID, please?" she asked.

I complied.

"May I ask the reason?" she asked softly. "I just need to put something here in the record for a chief complaint."

"I'm having a bad day," I cried. The situation was obviously a lot more complicated, but I suddenly felt that I just couldn't do it anymore and didn't know what else to say.

Other than the truth, which was that I needed help.

CHAPTER 9

Optics

July 2020, Outpatient Rehabilitation Center, Hawaii

Spring flowed into summer. I was beyond broken from months of grief. Anger. Rage. I was disgusted with myself. It all weighed down on me. Couldn't sleep or eat right. Nothing other than junk food was appetizing. I wanted to escape but didn't know how. Only thing I knew to do was seek refuge in a civilian outpatient psychiatric intensive program. I petitioned for medical leave.

Being treated at a different hospital meant everything because I knew nearly all of the residents and nurses at Main Hospital. My new safe haven was like daycare for mentally ill people. I immediately realized how helpful this robust approach could be. My new peers could be seen as weird and different—I fit right in.

I was ready to work the program and commit fully to therapy, except for one thing—I didn't want to confess that I was a doctor. My being there felt like such an admission of failure, and I just wanted to be a regular crazy person, if that concept exists.

The tension between my emotional low point and the veneer of external success seemed too difficult to explain. The struggle of balancing these optics was part of the reason I put off finding help for so long. Most high-achieving people around me that I grew to know so well didn't want to be seen as weak, or didn't allow themselves to falter. Although I appreciated this pattern in others, I didn't acknowledge it in myself.

In group therapy, I realized that I had never even allowed myself to grieve my father's death. I jumped right into my wedding, intern year, then salvaging Paul's career. Working to ignore the deepest grief I had ever experienced. All of that pain and sadness had grown into an angry ball of fire within me. I thought I was compartmentalizing, but instead, I was fueling rage and terror.

All it did was burn me from the inside out. Eventually, the fire died, leaving me an empty shell full of ashes, pushing away everyone I loved. My relationships with Paul, my mom, and Kyle lay in tatters because I had devoted so much time and energy to my seemingly endless problems at work. My last years with my family were non-existent because of medical school, and I will never get that time back. This vast sea of guilt reflected my past back to me, haunting me day in and day out.

All I had left to lose at that point was my sanity.

I sat there in the circle, grief overflowing, looking at my peers in group therapy. Everyone so uniquely different. Some reported that they had been diagnosed with bipolar, others, schizophrenia, others, drug addiction and dependency, and many others with depression or anxiety. Some suffering from a combination of the above.

Even though I was full to the brim with pain and suffering, I only had the courage to say, "I'm here because I don't get along well with my co-workers."

Optics

I owed the entire group the truth. I owed myself the truth.

But it was a start.

* * *

September 2020, Hawaii

Two months into my outpatient program, my mom called. I hadn't heard from her in a while, so I figured something was wrong. She was out of the loop on the shitshow of my life. I hadn't told her that Paul and I were so dismantled, or that I had gone through remediation and probation with residency now on the line.

I figured the less she knew about me, the less she could use against me when she felt like lashing out. I winced as I thought about her saying, "This is why nobody loves you or even likes you. Everyone knows you're a failure."

If she knew about all of the bureaucratic trouble I was facing, she'd tell me, "This is why you'll never make it as a surgeon." This was my biggest fear and the absolute last thing I wanted to hear, either then or whenever she decided to pull the pin and explode that comment in my face.

"Kyle is in the ER. He jumped. He jumped from the top of the stairs, Cindy," she cried. "He did it on purpose."

I could barely make sense of it. Guilt washed over me. I was reminded of how I made a mistake neglecting my father's health, believing things were fine because I hadn't heard otherwise. Now my brother. "Where is he?"

"Side's."

"I'm going." I pulled my depressed self together and grabbed my Side's ID.

* * *

Kyle grew up with childhood asthma. We called the nebulizer "the machine." He used it twice a day, sometimes with me holding the mask when he was too tired. This was my first exposure to the medical field—that and the unfinished house overflowing with OBGYN supplies my family sold.

Mom was a little disappointed when I told her I wanted to be an ENT. Not sure she ever understood it was still surgery. She wanted me to deliver babies. In hindsight, maybe she was onto something.

People would ask, "Why ENT?" My go-to response was that I wanted to be a Beverly Hills plastic surgeon. But who knows, maybe Kyle's asthma played a role.

As time went on though, my love and passion for medicine started fading away—like Kyle's childhood asthma. And it was getting harder and harder to figure out what I cared about anymore.

* * *

Optics

The ER at Side's was levels above the worn, familiar halls of Main Hospital. Everything gleamed with a sterile efficiency—from the freshly painted walls, polished floors, rolling computer kiosks—the faint whiff of rubbing alcohol.

I was led to a curtained-off corner where Kyle lay on a gurney, in a checkered hospital gown. An IV snaked into his arm. His hands and legs were scraped and bruised.

A nurse with a warm smile and a local accent approached me. "You Kyle's sister?" he asked, his voice gentle and reassuring.

"Yes," I choked out, tears welling up in my eyes.

"He's okay, just a little banged up. We're running some tests, but he seems to be alright."

I nodded, grateful for his kindness.

"Can I see him?" I asked, just steps away from Kyle. I needed him to know that he wasn't alone.

"Of course," the nurse replied, pulling back the curtain. "He's been asking for you."

I rushed to Kyle's side, taking his hand in mine. "Kyle, what happened? What did you do?"

His eyelids fluttered open, and he croaked out my name.

"Yes, Kyle, it's me. Your sister. I love you. Squeeze my hand."

He responded weakly, his grip surprisingly strong.

The ER doctor walked in, and I quickly composed myself, wiping away my tears. "Hi, I'm his sister. I'm an ENT resident at Main Hospital. Does he have any injuries? Is his C-spine cleared?"

"We just reviewed all the imaging. We can take the collar off now. He's very lucky, you know. He fell about twenty-five feet. Not sure why, but according to the report, he jumped. They think he was on PCP. It took four officers to hold him down. We're running the tox screen now."

"What? No!" I shook my head. PCP? Until that point, I was pretty sure that my brother only smoked weed. *Only.*

"We are having him evaluated by a psychiatrist, too," the doctor said. "Probably going to see if we can get him admitted to the psych ward. Your mother... Lynn, is it?"

"Yes."

"She's been calling, asking to see him, but we have a very strict visitor policy right now due to Covid." He looked at my badge, then added, "We made an exception for you, but typically we wouldn't allow family back here."

"Thank you so much. He feels so alone right now, I can tell." Even as I said it, though, I wondered how well I really knew my own brother. The distance between us had grown over the years, a rift widened by his brief stint in the Marines, dropping out of college, and the ever-present addiction issues clouding his relationship problems—on the surface, Kyle and I were so different.

"Your mother says he's been acting violent and erratic the last few months, and she's asking for him to be admitted. But he has no injuries. His other labs are all normal, pending the tox results. He has no known medical problems. The only way we could admit him would be for psychiatric reasons, pending an evaluation."

"What do you think?" I asked, wanting to defer to his expertise. Even this doctor, who had never met my mother, seemed to suspect she was overreacting.

"I've consulted them, and, as I'm sure you know, they are busy but will see him as soon as they can. Now, you're welcome to stay until they eval him—or we can call you."

"Um, I'll stay here for a bit, and then I'll give him his privacy and leave my number with you, if that's okay. My mom is his medical decision-maker, correct?"

"Yes."

I sat in the ER with Kyle for a couple hours, then left after he drifted off to sleep, still waiting for his consult. As I walked back out into the humid evening, I found myself in complete disbelief. My mom and I fought about his drug habits over the years. She was always in denial. Our explosive blowout fights resulted in months of no contact.

I realized that I was jealous of Kyle. His coping mechanisms. He didn't have my responsibilities. If he felt stressed, he could numb out and forget his problems. I was failing to balance my emotions and mental health struggles.

Meanwhile, going to therapy. Doing my best to be more self-aware.

My desire to become a surgeon eclipsed everything else. Stone-cold sober, I had no choice but to look life and its challenges in the face. No blissful escapes.

Kyle was one of those challenges. The number of times I tried to tell my mom that he was on drugs. Was this jump the thing that would make her face the truth?

Addiction tends to swallow the addict, and whoever is in their orbit, whole. I knew that creating and maintaining boundaries was healthy, but this was my brother. My blood.

I left the ER that night with a heavy, conflicted heart, wondering all over again whether I was doing enough. Whether I was enough.

* * *

September 2020, Hawaii

When I got home and told Paul about Kyle, the generic apology about how things were hard with my family didn't feel sincere.

"How long is your leave going to be?" he asked, changing the subject.

"I don't know, Paul. As long as I need. Why?"

Optics

"When is the hearing?"

"Main Hospital hasn't done one during Covid yet, so nobody knows the protocol."

"It's been months since they gave you the proposal, Cindy. What are you going to do when you go back? They're not going to treat you the same. They won't let you operate at Side's, they won't let you take solo call, they won't give you cases at Main. They aren't going to graduate you!!"

"Don't ever say that again!! Don't manifest that!"

"Be realistic, Cindy. Can't you see what they're doing? The longer you go without signing the proposal, the worse it looks for you. You need to get back at them. File complaints. Go to the hospital commander. Blow the whistle on the cheating. Go to NCRA. Go to NBO. File an IG complaint. File a Congressional inquiry!!"

"Well, you know what? Maybe I will, Paul. Maybe I will. Maybe I'll even write a book, too, and tell my story. But you know what's ironic? You preach about this, but you did NOTHING for yourself. I had to do it for you. I had to tell you to apply for residency. Without me, where would you be?"

Paul grabbed his keys and walked out. I poured myself a glass of wine and sat on the balcony, looking at the city lights and listening to the ever-present hush of the ocean. I barely wondered where Paul was going or when—if—he would be back. He was gone so often now that I had no idea where he went anymore. Or who he was.

TOO MUCH

I was tempted to text him, but I didn't.

When I woke up in the middle of the night with a terrible feeling in the pit of my stomach, he was still gone.

* * *

September 2020, Side's Hospital, Hawaii

As soon as my group therapy session concluded the next day, I raced to Side's to see Kyle. My mom was sitting in the waiting area, looking tired, withdrawn.

"Can we go in to see Kyle?" I asked, wondering why she wasn't in with him already.

"He wants to see you first. He doesn't want to see me yet."

They escorted me back and he was wearing scrubs like mine, but in prison beige. A stark reminder that nothing really separated me from the patients inside the psychiatric ward, except maybe privilege and one breakdown. The guard walked me to the common area. There were several men scattered throughout, some reading or writing, some just sitting quietly, and others talking to themselves.

"Kyle!" I gave him a hug and held back from crying.

"Want to sit?" He gestured at a table with two chairs in the corner of the recreation room. "Cindy, I saw Dad," he whispered in a confessional tone. His eyes were puffy and red.

Optics

"What do you mean?"

"Dad, he's been talking to me. He's Jesus."

"Kyle, don't say that."

"Yes, and I saw the devil in the mango tree. Cindy, it started flying around the house, and it was gonna hurt Mom, so that's why I was trying to kill it with the baseball bat. It kept going around the house everywhere. And"—he started crying—"I saw my best friend, Cindy."

"Who?"

"The one that died, from Marine training."

Kyle didn't talk much about his short stint in the Marines, so it didn't surprise me that he apparently had a best friend that I'd never heard of.

"He got into a motorcycle accident. In Texas. He died a week before Dad did."

I just sat there. The motorcycle friend seemed plausible because, unfortunately, the military tended to lose a lot of young people to off-duty, highly risky behavior. But did Kyle actually believe that he saw Dad? Or that Dad was Jesus? And did he tear the house apart with a baseball bat because he saw the devil?

Mom had texted me photos of the damage, but I hadn't yet gathered the courage to go see it for myself. Kyle smashed his computer, his closet, his bedroom door, and the kitchen floor. He left deep gouges in the drywall. After the frenzy, he jumped to the bottom of the garage stairs.

"Can Mom come visit?" I asked, gently.

"Yeah, but only if you promise you'll get me out of here, Cindy."

"I will do my best, but the final call is up to the doctors. They're going to make you take some medicine. Promise me you'll listen to them, okay?"

"I'll do anything but I can't stay here." He lowered his voice and looked around. "Cindy, the people here are crazy."

* * *

The hospital changes after the sun sets. When the traumas come out, stories get weirder and weirder.

While tourists skip around Waikiki paying extra fees for parking and Mai Tais, a deeply rooted drug and sex trafficking world thrives underground. At least half of the trauma patients I saw on call had gotten rolled up in the wrong lifestyle with no honest way out. They seemed disconnected, missing all but one or two teeth, covered in scabs, fresh wounds, and scrapes. Often with a "boyfriend" or "girlfriend" at their bedsides.

"She seems quite lethargic?" I asked a nurse the first time I saw this play out.

"Oh, that's normal. It's been three days, so she's coming down. She doesn't need anything."

"I can't wake her up…" I insisted.

"No, it's just the meth, honey." the nurse smiled as if I was clueless. I guess, *I was.*

We didn't even bother drug testing them unless we were planning to operate.

We refined our surgical plan for meth users because we had learned that *meth mouth* impacted wound healing. It was more beneficial to repair their fractures through a neck incision—the wound would otherwise breakdown if we tried a less "invasive" approach intraorally.

The veil between the woman in the bed, Kyle, and me seemed so thin. To be taking care of *other* drug addicts, as if I was superior. Was I?

My colleagues and I joked "meth mouth," but deep down, I was no different.

Dr. Bates once said to me, "I'm surprised you made it this far."

Me too.

* * *

1990s Hawaii

Kyle and I would spend hours outside our house. We'd stack

cinderblocks, transforming them, hollow them out to hide our treasures, and rearrange them into ever-changing landscapes. The rough, gray blocks were our jumbo-sized Legos, the blank canvas for our imaginations.

Looking back, I'm still amazed that our parents let us play unsupervised amidst the construction debris. Perhaps they were too exhausted from their long workdays to care, or maybe they understood the value of unstructured play in our sprawling, unfinished backyard. To us, the cinderblocks were a source of endless fascination, their potential limited only by our creativity.

But as I grew older, the novelty of our makeshift playground wore off. The sight of the unfinished house, its exposed beams and gaping holes, began to fill me with a gnawing sense of shame. I longed for the manicured lawns and pristine homes of my friends' and neighbors, a stark contrast to our own chaotic and incomplete dwelling.

The unfinished house became a silent witness to our family's struggles, a constant reminder of the dreams deferred and the sacrifices made. It was a monument to my parents' unwavering determination to provide for their children, even if it meant living in a perpetual state of incompleteness.

* * *

September 2020, Hawaii

Before Kyle was going to be discharged back home, I needed to see what had happened. He had taken his baseball bat to his computer, to the walls, to his closet. My mom had done her best to clean everything up—the shattered computer, the splintered wooden dresser drawers, the hole in the bedroom door. The entire scene was terrifying. I took photos because I couldn't believe it was real. How could Kyle do this? What happened? Was it the drugs?

I searched his room and grabbed the bongs and drugs. I got a large trash bag and started dumping everything.

"No, Cindy! He's going to be so upset!"

"Are you *kidding me*?" I couldn't help my anger. "*This*"—I swept my arm around and I screamed at the top of my lungs — "is why he went off. These fucking drugs. I've been telling you about it for years and years and years. Ever since he was fourteen. You never wanted to listen to me! And look what happened! Do you want him to die next time? Do you want him to kill you?!"

I grabbed the baseball bat, and she recoiled, but then I shoved it into the bag. "Where is anything else he can use as a weapon? Show me now!"

"He has a knife," Mom said, wiping at her tears and trembling.

"I'm taking it, and then we are calling the cops to take ALL OF THIS FUCKING SHIT away, because I'm not putting it in my car or the trash. I'm in the Army, and I'm not going to be responsible for people going through your trash and overdosing on his shit."

My mom collapsed into my arms, crying. Years of unfailing love for my brother, years of appeasement and denial, had led to this. It wasn't her fault, but I knew she thought it was. I hugged her. Poor Lynn.

Her hair was plastered to her face, wet from tears, hot from rage. She was smaller than me, trembling in my arms. It was almost like she was the child, and I the mother—a dynamic that I deeply resented, but learned to accept. Because more than anything in the world, I knew she loved us.

I knew she was sorry. And in this weird, sick, strange way, if I could have changed anything about Lynn—I wouldn't. As much as we had been through, the nasty fights, the texts, the emails, I loved my mother. No matter what. No matter how crazy and psychotic she got. Sounds toxic. But maybe that's what love is. I don't know.

Later that day, my brother was discharged from Side's, and Mom was too afraid to pick him up. We went to get ice cream and sat in the parking lot.

"Kyle," I started, "it's okay to be like this. I'm like this, too. And so was Dad. We just have different brain chemistry and more to deal with. But we can make it."

"Yeah?" he said.

"You just need to take your medication, okay?"

It was ironic that I was telling him to take medication when I had been on and off my own for years. Figuring out the right dosing and formulation of psychiatric medication was such a long and dehumanizing process. I wasn't sure I could reach a successful solution for myself, and relief seemed downright impossible for someone as volatile as Kyle. I worried he'd be back to his old ways in a matter of days, if not hours.

Optics

My mind was racing as I drove him back to my mom's house, but there was nowhere else for Kyle to go—as much as I loved my brother—for a split second I considered it— there was no way he could stay with me and Paul. I dropped Kyle off and made him promise that he'd take his meds... continued on my way back home. Remembered the fight with Paul.

When I unlocked the door of our condo, Paul was sitting on the couch, eating leftover pizza like nothing happened.

"Where the fuck were you all night?"

"Nowhere."

"Are you kidding me? Kyle has been in the hospital, and you fucking vanish? Where did you go?"

"Fine. If you must know, I went to a strip club."

I rushed to the junk drawer in the kitchen, grabbed a permanent marker and wrote on the walls:

PAUL FUCKS WHORES

PAUL IS A LIAR

PAUL FUCKS STRIPPERS

FUCK YOU CHEATING ASSHOLE

"What the fuck are you doing?" Paul raised his voice.

"Fuck you, asshole." I threw the marker on the ground and slammed the bedroom door.

I was done. Done with everything and everyone.

I didn't care if the cops came again. I had already seen them once that day to hand off Kyle's shit. They knew my mom's house.

I was on their radar in two different neighborhoods and I didn't care.

* * *

November 2020, Hawaii

In spite of my interpersonal conflicts, I graduated from the outpatient program with flying colors and even got a certificate to prove it. Unfortunately, this also meant that my medical leave was over. Back to residency.

For additional support, I continued the mental health program on a less intensive schedule. On Friday afternoons, kept my pager on vibration mode, still hiding my identity as a doctor. Found a sneaky solution by forwarding my pages to my upper residents.

Dr. Bates got wind of that and mandated me to drive back and forth for calls. Eventually, this got to be too much, so I dropped out. Weekly visits with Dr. Owens became my only support system.

Over time, Dr. Owens and I built rapport, talking about various things, such as how it had been over six months since I got any feed-back in writing from my attendings. I was still in the midst of waiting for the probation hearing because of Covid, and my attorney was backlogged with all the state's cases that had been put on hold.

Because of all the waiting and anxiety that came along with it, I eventually said f-it and agreed to probation, though I objected that slamming a door was grounds. This felt like just one step closer to my inevitable fate. We were conducting all of our academic sessions online, and I wasn't operating. I started buying and reselling luxury goods online to pass the time, in an echo of Paul's stint with rideshare.

* * *

December 2020, Main Hospital, Hawaii

The hospital adjusted to Covid. We were back to operating a few times a week with clinics open again. Tony abruptly returned to Main Hospital from his rotation at Side's. This messed up the entire call schedule—and he took some of my cases as the "senior" resident.

"Why are you back?" I asked him directly.

"Ughhhh," he moaned. "I don't want to talk about it."

I asked around and heard that he'd pissed off Dr. Cole at Side's in-traoperatively, though I could never confirm first-hand what ex-actly happened. Yet, everyone loved to gossip about my professional shortcomings.

He flashed a sexy grin at me and brushed my shoulder, "but the good news is, at least I can actually operate here. And not have to fudge the numbers. You know what I mean? I need cases."

I flashed a forced smile back. Even though it was a major double standard. Tony was sent back to Main Hospital, taking my head and neck cases because he "needed them." *I needed them.*

I was written up for not wearing a badge and placed on remediation for my tone of voice and facial expressions. Then I allegedly slammed a broken door, and that was the last straw? *But Tony could still operate and round on patients?*

Tony played nice-nice in the sandbox as the "hot, pretty doctor," so everyone in my residency looked past his f-ups. Everyone else cheating their way to the top. None of the attendings seemed to care.

When I realized that Tony was getting a glorified slap on the wrist from Dr. Bates and nothing else, I snapped.

Fuck it.

Everything I'd experienced in the last few months came to a head and clicked into frightening clarity. I threw open my work laptop and found the hospital commander's email. She had an open-door policy.

Paul was right.

I wrote an email, explaining the cheating situation, attaching Isaac's Google doc, citing examples of gender discrimination with photos of soft-core porn novels I'd already complained about in years past to Dr. Bates.

Optics

"We'll talk to the other residents about that," Dr. Bates and Dr. Pratt had reassured me. I snapped photos of all those books regardless. Deep down, part of me knew this day was always coming.

I hit "send."

Deep down, I knew that I was doing something I could never take back.

I looked up the contact information for the National Board of Otolaryngology. Cited their cheating policy. "Send."

Part of me was doing it out of anger.

Vengeance.

And then, the liaison to email a formal complaint to the National Council, citing all the residency violations. "Send."

Part of me knew I could never look back.

Part of me knew my career would never be the same.

Part of me wondered if I would ever have any career at all after this.

But I fantasized about doing this for so long, that sending these emails felt good.

Finally, I could be free.

Because the truth is that Main Hospital ENT—"number one in the nation"—was not number one. Not so professional. Not so rigorous. All I witnessed was a fucking clique. An afterparty. A show.

Even though I knew I deserved better—that this residency was never the place for me, that I would never be trained the way I should be—my inner sense of justice and integrity wouldn't let me just walk away. Not after all of these years of working.

Not after walking away from my past dreams for the rest of my life.

No. This wasn't about becoming an ENT anymore.

This was about proving them all wrong.

I was done failing to play the game by their rules.

I was playing my own game now.

CHAPTER 10

Numbers

January 2021, Main Hospital, Hawaii

Suzy, with her sparkling green eyes peeking above her mask and a halo of ginger red hair escaping her surgical cap, bopped around the clinic. Even when she talked down to "subordinates," her singsong voice and wide-eyed innocence made it hard to take offense. She mastered the perfect calibration where helpless meets friendly.

Despite her seemingly perfect façade, Suzy made mistakes—all residents do. She was rarely scrutinized, while I lived under the microscope. As my senior resident, Suzy held power over me. Any miscommunication from my end could be interpreted as insubordination. It was a frustrating dynamic, especially when we socialized outside of work. Her drunk alter-ego, "Suze," was a wild card.

After the attendings clocked out, residents were left to handle minor procedures. This included biopsies, small mass removals, and even our "underground" Botox and filler services. However, during the pandemic, these procedures came to a halt due to nationwide shortages.

Healthcare was crumbling before our eyes. Doctors and nurses, lured by lucrative travel positions, were abandoning their posts. Main Hospital was hemorrhaging staff. The Army's solution was to siphon personnel from our already depleted ranks to fill the gaps at other facilities. It was a frustrating situation, especially considering Main Hospital's critical role as one of only two trauma centers in the state, serving a vast population, including underserved communities on neighboring islands.

One day in the procedure clinic, Suzy was performing a nasal biopsy on a patient. I offered to assist, but she declined with a smile that felt more like a dismissal than a polite refusal. Later that afternoon, I discovered that the specimen label printer was broken, forcing us to manually label the sample.

The following Friday, during our academic session, Dr. Bates called in the techs to announce that one of Suzy's specimens had been lost. The department had to contact the patient to see if there was any remaining tissue for a repeat biopsy, as we were trying to rule out cancer.

Suzy, with her wide eyes and innocent demeanor, chimed in, "Honestly, I really don't think it was cancer. I think it was just a papilloma."

Dr. Bates turned to me and said, "Make sure you're in the room, Cindy, and label the cup yourself, so we don't have another incident."

I couldn't help myself from being jealous of Suzy. Strawberry Shortcake Suzy didn't seem to have a care in the world. She could lose a specimen and the next day, a new department policy! Everything was rainbows and sunshine for Suze. I was unhinged, to say the least.

* * *

Numbers

Paul found a cheap rental after I flipped out redecorating our walls. He didn't tell me where he was living because he thought I was going to show up and destroy that place, too. We were planning to renovate the condo, so I didn't feel that bad about taking a marker to the wall or ripping out the bookshelves.

But looking back, I realize that it wasn't a healthy way to express my anger or frustration over our disintegrating marriage. Instead of working together, we retreated into our own coping mechanisms—Paul with alcohol and late nights out, and me with work and self-blame. We were both hurting, and it created a toxic cycle of resentment and misunderstanding.

"Paul," I begged him on the phone a few weeks after he left, "please come home."

"No, Cindy. It's not safe for me there. You're not safe right now. You need help."

I was still adjusting to my medication, and, even though I felt more level-headed, Paul wanted more time and space. Neither of us was getting any of our needs met, and our relationship—what was left of it—felt like a lost cause.

"Paul, you don't understand. It's getting worse. The program is out to get me. And I don't know when this stupid investigation is going to start, when the probation hearing is going to happen, or what I should do next. They're watching me all the time. I feel everyone talking about me. Whenever I walk by, people stop whispering.

"People laugh at me. One of the scrub techs told me the other day that people gossip about me, that I'm a bitch. I don't know what to say. I try to keep quiet. Paul, I hung a blanket around my desk because I'm scared of people looking at me. I don't want to make eye contact because of my resting bitch face."

"Cindy, I told you, ask them to transfer you to another program." He sounded genuinely concerned, even though his distance made it hard to fully believe him.

"I don't know if they'll do that now with the investigation happening."

In the weeks since I'd sent the emails, I vacillated between terror that they'd take my complaints seriously, and hopelessness that they wouldn't. By this point, there had been a response—but it was strictly procedural.

I met with the Deputy Commander of the hospital, and was assigned an Investigating Officer, Dr. James, the OBGYN Program Director.

"You had to send those emails," Paul said, his voice a mix of frustration and worry.

Paul was the one who told me to stand up for myself, and now he found something else to criticize. "I did. And they're actually responding. I don't want to get my hopes up, but I have to see it through."

"Is your attorney going to be there?"

"No. I don't know about him. He never got back to me about the probation hearing. And besides, I don't have that kind of money right now. Speaking of which, I need your half of the mortgage.

"You're the one who wanted the renovations. And you're the one who fucked up the walls, Cindy. I'll send you half." He paused, his voice softening slightly. "You ready for the in-service exam?"

I hated this pattern that we kept falling into, the same few fights about career and imbalanced support and money. It made me wonder what our connection was when we were first falling in love.

"I can't even think about the test."

"Just do your best, Cindy. Who cares? I didn't study last year, and I scored in the fiftieth percentile. Think about it. If we don't study and score in the middle of all the residents in the country, that's not bad. We are average among really smart people."

"I'm not smart," I added under my breath.

"You're competing against residents at institutions like Harvard and Mayo and UCSF, and you aren't even trying. Don't let them make you feel bad about it. It's just a number." He tried to reassure me, but his words felt hollow. The distance between us was growing wider with each passing day.

* * *

TOO MUCH

Lance, the scrub tech, moved like a well-oiled machine, his hands a blur as he draped the tubes across the mayo stand.

"Dr. Neighbors likes it this way," he told Nick, nodding in my direction. I offered a grateful smile, finding comfort in the familiarity of his routine.

As we moved through the pre-op team briefing, my anxiety began to subside, replaced by a familiar focus. The rhythmic beeping of the heart monitor, the hiss of the oxygen tank, the clinking of instruments—these were the sounds of my world, my sanctuary.

Nick, to his credit, was a quick learner. He was soon on his way to removing the first tonsil without any issues, his movements precise and confident. I stepped back to observe, my eyes scanning the surgical field for any potential complications. That's when I saw Jefferson, the new scrub nurse, fumbling with the bovie cord, her hands shaking.

"Don't touch that," I said, placing my hand on the cord to steady it. My eyes remained fixed on the patient's mouth, ensuring the surgery continued smoothly. The rest of the procedure went off without a hitch. Dr. Tam, the supervising attending, reappeared just as we were finishing up, as if he had been present the entire time.

As we wheeled the patient out of the OR, a military police officer approached me. "Captain Neighbors," he said, his voice a low rumble that sent a shiver down my spine. "Dr. Bates is asking for you downstairs."

Dread pooled in my stomach. "Right now?" I asked. "I have another surgery to start."

"Dr. Tam and Nick can handle that," the officer said, his tone leaving no room for argument. He turned and walked briskly down the hallway.

I followed, my heart pounding in my chest. Two military police officers were waiting in the ENT conference room, their bulletproof vests and holsters gleaming under the fluorescent lights

"Captain Neighbors?" one of the officers asked.

"Yes," I replied.

"We received a report that you physically assaulted a member of the operating room staff this morning."

The words hit me like a physical blow. Assault?

As the officer continued, detailing the accusation, my mind began to race. It was a setup, I was sure of it. They were trying to silence me. They were trying to destroy me.

A wave of paranoia threatening to drown me in its dark depths. I wanted to scream, to run, to disappear. But I stood my ground, my body frozen in place, my mind a maelstrom of fear and disbelief.

The solider wrote my number in his notebook and handed me his card. In a daze, I slowly walked out of the conference room. I passed Dr. Bates's office, and my company commander, Captain Roberts, was there. They both just stared. The last thing I wanted was to pop in and ask questions. I was speechless, confused, mortified.

People could spread rumors or complain about my tone all they wanted, but assault? That was serious. Especially in the Army. An assault conviction had turned Paul's life into a dumpster fire. Now I stood accused of the same.

The wheels spun in my head, and the downward paranoid spiral continued. This had to be a set-up. Because I'd sent the emails. They had it out for me from the beginning. Because my husband lost his Urology spot. Because he was convicted. Because I stole Paul in the first place. Because I was a homewrecking whore.

Because because because.

It was all coming back to haunt me. My mother was right. I *was* bad, and I was going to pay for it all. That had to be the only explanation.

* * *

March 2021, Hawaii

Accused of assaulting a scrub tech, I was swiftly removed from the program. Dr. Bates had found a loophole, expertly navigating the system to sideline me without due process. The timing was impeccable: with Covid restrictions lifted, they convened a three-hour, court-style hearing attended by fifty influential figures in the medical community.

The focus? An endless replay of the alleged altercation, an event I was still trying to comprehend. I had four witnesses on my side, all confirming they hadn't seen me assault anyone. Dr. Tam, the attending, was conspicuously absent.

Dr. Bates had his own witness, an OR nurse who wasn't even present during the incident. She recounted a secondhand story of the alleged victim, Specialist Jefferson, claiming I had slapped her hand. Jefferson herself was nowhere to be found.

The hearing felt like a mockery of justice, a witch trial designed to oust me. Later that evening, Dr. Kent called to deliver the verdict: suspension. They had no evidence of the assault, but crucially, no evidence to disprove it either. Guilty by default.

The decision stung, a deep betrayal by the very people who were supposed to mentor and guide me. It was a stark reminder that in this system, truth and justice were often secondary to power and politics.

* * *

March 2021, Hawaii

They still hadn't wrapped up the hospital investigation about the cheating scandal. Dr. James called me after the hearing to inquire about my availability for an interview in her office.

The first thing I noticed in her office was her large Birkin, atop a stack of patient charts. She was a reproductive-and-endocrinology-fellowship-trained OBGYN, and her husband was also a surgeon on the island.

God only knows what else she knew.

The longer I went without any news on the assault allegation, the less I believed anyone would care or do anything. I regretted sending all the emails. I knew what I was feeling when I did it, but I was so used to second-guessing myself that I had no sense of right or wrong anymore. And then it dawned on me, did she—did the *hospital*—even know I sent the other emails out?

"Cindy, we want you to know that the hospital commander took your concerns about the cheating very seriously. I spent a lot of time reviewing all of the material you sent, and we are going to interview every single person in the ENT department. Starting with you. Now. We have a lot of questions here." She slid a packet over.

I couldn't believe it. The hospital had finally listened.

"I don't expect you to answer these today, or even this week. Take your time. I'll need a typed-up official statement, for the record. It will be considered in our investigation. Just remember, this is an official sworn statement, so everything you submit has to be true to the best of your recollection."

"I understand."

"Do you have any questions?"

"Do the other residents…will they know who reported everything?"

"No, Cindy. Everything you submitted to us will remain confidential, but we do have to ask questions about the issues you raised. If you turn to page two, you will see that we've identified concerns about the cheating, the sexual harassment allegations, and discrimination in the workplace. We will be asking the individuals you cited in your email about their version of events. They might wonder who made the report, but we certainly won't be naming you."

I sat wondering, *Could I take it all back?*

I could say I made it all up.

More and more, it seemed that the whistleblowing would just be met with more blow-back. Everything I did was just being used against me.

I wanted NBO to investigate. I wanted someone to take my concerns seriously, but to what expense?

Could we just start over again?

Could we pretend none of this ever happened?

I questioned myself, the things that I once knew to be true.

Not only had I run out of options, I was now clinging to the last ounce of my own sanity and credibility.

I hit the road where desperation meets panic…survival.

CHAPTER 11

Thanks

March 2021, Main Hospital, Hawaii

"Something operations." It sounded fancy but was only staffed by two people: a secretary and Major Ernst. When Major Ernst asked why I'd been assigned to work under him as a fourth-year ENT resident, I was too tired to pretend.

"I was accused of assaulting someone in the OR," I answered. "They suspended me from clinical responsibilities, but since I'm still getting paid, they need me to report for duty in one way or another. Nobody has charged me or arrested me, and there's no pending legal action, so I don't know how long I'll be here."

Major Ernst, a crisply dressed officer with a quiet intensity, raised an eyebrow. "Nobody has contacted you?"

I shook my head, the weight of the past few weeks pressing down on me. "No. It's been a nightmare."

He nodded slowly, a thoughtful expression on his face. "Well, I'm Major Ernst. Welcome! It's not exactly the OR, but we'll make the best of it."

In the following days, Major Ernst and I fell into an unexpected camaraderie. We filled the hours between his internet conferences with conversations about everything from the hospital's budget woes to my writing dreams. He was a good listener, offering a sympathetic ear and a fresh perspective on the challenges I faced.

One day, as we discussed my stalled writing projects, Major Ernst surprised me with a bold suggestion. "Screw that fictional novel," he said, his voice firm. "Write *your* story. The real one. Use people's real names. Expose the truth about what's happening in the residency program. People need to know."

His words hung in the air, a challenge and a lifeline. A warmth spread through my chest, a flicker of hope I hadn't felt in months. *Write my story? Expose the truth?* A part of me thrilled at the thought of defiance, of reclaiming my narrative. Then the doubts. *Who would believe me? What if they retaliate? What if it destroys my career...whatever is left of it?*

"How can I write about my own life without backlash?" I asked. "Nobody will believe me."

"They will," he insisted. "Your story is important. It's a story of resilience, of fighting against a broken system. It's a story that needs to be told."

I began to see my experiences not as a source of shame, but as a catalyst for change. I started outlining my story, the words flowing onto the page with a newfound urgency.

But even as I wrote, a nagging fear lingered. Would speaking out cost me everything? My career, my reputation, my sanity? The stakes were high, but the desire for justice burned even brighter.

One afternoon, as I was immersed in my writing, Major Ernst interrupted me with a question. "Have you received the findings from the assault investigation?"

I looked up, startled. "What investigation?" I had almost forgotten about the incident in the OR, overshadowed by the NBO inquiry and my own emotional turmoil.

"The 15-6," he explained. "It's a standard report filed after any investigation. You have a right to see it."

His words sent a jolt of adrenaline through me. Could this be the key to clearing my name? To proving that the assault accusation was a fabrication?

I researched how to file a Freedom of Information Act request, my heart pounding with a mix of hope and trepidation. The truth, it seemed, was within reach. But would it set me free, or would it only drag me deeper into the abyss?

* * *

March 2021, Hawaii

I was starting to accept my new life as a failure: a failed wife, a failed ENT surgical resident, and a failed aspiring writer.

I'd achieved a small victory by convincing Paul to move back into the renovated condo. We had new turquoise mosaic glass kitchen back-splash tiles, white quartz countertops, and plank wooden floors. The walls were also freshly painted, covering up my "manic episode."

Then I got an email:

> Congratulations. The hospital commander approved the appeal of your suspension. You may return to the ENT department on Monday.

I couldn't believe it. One person. One person ruled in my favor against a committee of over fifty other decision-makers at the hospital. I read the email again and began to weep. My bogus suspension had been overturned. Someone at the top saw how ridiculous it was.

I felt utterly vindicated! This unexpected change in my luck was so shocking that I couldn't believe it was real.

What kind of existence was this? When something devastating happened, I couldn't believe it. When a miracle happened, I couldn't believe it, either.

Paul was shocked. "Wow, it really means something for the hospital commander to reverse the decision, Cindy. All of those attendings voted against you, and *bam*."

I allowed myself to hope that I could actually get back into the program and become an ENT, after all. That someone saw my worth, and that I wasn't actually crazy.

When I went back to work on Monday, the attendings were acting unusually nice to me. It didn't quite add up, but I didn't want to continue questioning everything, so I pretended not to be weirded out.

I met with Dr. Owens, as usual, and wondered whether we'd talk about the suspension, or the larger issue of the program probation, which was still in effect. "Crazy few weeks, huh?" I asked, trying to make light of the situation.

"It certainly was." Dr. Owens smiled, tightly. I wondered whether she was with me or against me on the assault. "But the issue of your probation remains. They aren't sure you're at the same level as your peers, and that's a problem for your graduation timeline."

I tried to lighten my tone of voice. "I mean, their position has always been about tone, not performance."

"Cindy, I understand you're frustrated. But maybe it's time to take the pressure off. Have you considered repeating your fourth year of residency?"

This wasn't the first I'd heard of this option. Dr. Owens phrased it as a choice, yet it seemed anything but. By framing it this way and pretending it was my idea, they probably wanted to save me the humiliation of proposing it myself.

Instead of over-thinking it, I took the hint. I headed downstairs and offered this idea to Dr. Bates, and he gladly accepted. Then I began the process of slowly telling people that I wouldn't become a chief resident with Steve in three months. So close, and yet so far.

Thanks

With this plan in place, at least I stood the chance of actually graduating.

* * *

April 2021, Hawaii

Once I settled into probation and accepted that I wouldn't be graduating on time, things improved. The virtual communication course I was required to take was surprisingly helpful. We were a diverse group, all mandated to be there for various reasons.

One man had been accused of sexual harassment. Another woman criticized for being soft-spoken. Interpersonal conflicts seemed universal, regardless of rank or experience. It was eye-opening to realize that even seasoned professionals faced discrimination and mistreatment. One Black female surgeon shared how she'd had to switch hospitals multiple times to escape bullying.

Despite the heavy stories, we focused on thriving in the face of adversity. At the end, I thanked my cohort for their kindness and support. Their impact on me was profound. When I shared the positive feedback with Dr. Bates, he was stunned:

> Of all the course participants, people felt closest to Dr. Neighbors, perhaps because it is difficult to see someone struggle at such a pivotal time in their career, but more likely because she was so genuine in expressing how hard it has been for her. We saw real progress in owning her triggers and how the assumptions that she was making about her colleagues created distance. Her Action Plan reflects a

detailed and humble desire to treat people better and to question her own role in relationship failure. She committed to looking at the words she uses, her body language and facial expressions to foster closer, more vulnerable connection to people.

Even though I wouldn't be graduating with my cohort, I felt, for the first time in a long while, that I could actually make it through residency.

* * *

May 2021, Main Hospital, Hawaii

Probation was going smoothly, and I was adjusting to the life of a "senior resident," complete with borrowing shoes from male colleagues and impromptu Botox sessions.

"Think I can get some Botox?" Jennifer asked one day.

"Sure," I shrugged, "let's go downstairs."

Despite the lighthearted moments, the underlying pressure of the program was always present. A seemingly routine ER consult for a facial laceration led to a brief connection with another doctor over a shared alma mater. However, the constant scrutiny of the program lingered, leaving me with the agonizing anticipation of waiting for the other shoe to drop.

I ran into Dr. Thatcher again—he stopped me in the hallway. Or I stopped him. I can't remember. It felt pointless to talk about the alleged assault, but I figured he heard about it from all the OR gossip.

"Long time no see, Cindy."

"Yeah," I smiled and shrugged. Shuffled my feet.

"How's everything going? Are you okay?"

"Yeah, I'm okay—why wouldn't I be?"

"You know, I can be your mentor, if you need one?"

"Oh, thanks. I guess, I kind of thought, that's why we talk sometimes."

"Sure, but you have my number? Just in case."

Dr. Thatcher gave me his cell. I knew he was being sincere about the offer to be a mentor and I tried not to overthink it, but I also remembered we should set boundaries. Paul had just moved back in. Dr. Thatcher was married. I was also probably on my way to exposing the entire hospital for all their lies and scandals and on my way to having absolutely no career, so it made no sense that all I could think about was his cute blue eyes. I thought about deleting his number. Instead, I changed the name to, "Dr. Mentor" as a reminder to myself.

* * *

May 2021, Main Hospital, Hawaii

That Friday in Academics, Dr. Bates came into the room with another announcement, which was now becoming routine. Every time I saw him, my entire body tightened involuntarily. *Would this be about me not being elevated to chief resident alongside Steve?*

"Hey, everyone, I just wanted to let you know that the hospital commander concluded an investigation into the department—"

Which investigation?

"—and we need to change a few policies here. First, we need to address something right away." Dr. Bates locked eyes with me, and my breath hitched in my chest.

"Starting this afternoon, if we take patient photos, we have to ask patients for their consent via a signed release form." He continued on with the explanation of the new protocol as multiple residents groaned.

"You can't even upload photos from the camera to the charts. The battery is always dead." Tony protested.

Jeff and Nick chimed in with their comments. I had nothing to say. Dr. Bates pressed forward with the new protocol. The room fell quiet, and I swore a few residents glanced my way.

"Okay, that's all I have." Dr. Bates said. He turned to walk out the room and everyone dreadfully gathered themselves to continue on with the day.

"Don't forget to RSVP to the graduation dinner, everyone!" Steve said.

Thanks

"Oh, yeah, thank you, Steve!" Dr. Bates said, with a beaming smile back at his favorite. *Steve.*

* * *

May 2021, Hawaii

We needed to escape the monotony of our lives, to recapture a spark from the past. We dressed up—me in my finest designer heels, a Chanel purse he'd gifted me years ago, and a little black dress; Paul in a more casual Aloha shirt and pants—ventured to a charming Italian restaurant.

Yet, even with a bottle of wine and forced smiles, the dinner felt hollow. We both glanced at our phones, avoiding the truth in each other's eyes. We booked a rideshare, opting for responsible choices in light of a recent hospital incident. But responsibility had a dangerous side. It made it easier to overindulge. Paul and I shared a love of impulsive highs, addicted to adrenaline, which masked the deeper issues in our marriage.

That night, the realization hit me—the thrill was gone, and I couldn't get it back. A wave of impulsivity and wine-fueled courage washed over me. I excused myself to the bathroom and, in a moment of reckless abandon, called Dr. Thatcher.

"Hi, it's Cindy," I stammered, already regretting the call.

"Hi," his voice was groggy, a reminder of the late hour.

"Um, I was wondering if we could talk."

"Right now?"

"Is your wife home?" I whispered, instantly regretting each word coming out of my mouth.

"She's on the mainland—working—why?"

"I mean, in a little bit. I'm finishing dinner. Can I come over when I'm done?"

In the bathroom mirror, I saw a stranger—a woman acting in desperation, seeking validation outside of her marriage. The wine made it all feel like a dream.

"Sure, just let me know when you're here," he replied.

I returned to the table, a mask of normalcy barely hiding my conflicting emotions of guilt and excitement.

Back at our condo, the silence was deafening. Paul retreated to the office with a beer, offering no affection, no acknowledgment of my efforts.

"I'm just gonna go to bed early tonight, Paul," I called out, a mix of resignation and defiance in my voice.

"Yup," he replied, shutting the door.

His indifference fueled my resolve. I slipped out of the condo, heart pounding, heels dangling from my finger as I raced across the street towards Dr. Thatcher's building. I called him, shamelessly asking him

Thanks

to buzz me in. He met me in the lobby, looking casual and confused. We exchanged awkward pleasantries as I put my heels back on, the lobby lights casting long, uncertain shadows.

If you're wondering how I know where Dr. Thatcher lived, it's not because I stalked him—it's because he casually mentioned it in the OR once. Just once, and that's all it took I guess, to plant the seed in my brain—of this all happening, someday. And I guess, that day—or night rather, was then and there.

"So, what did you want to talk about?" he asked, his tone cautious.

"Um, it's kind of private, actually," I stumbled, trying to regain my composure. "Can we go up to your place?"

My heart sank. This wasn't the fantasy I conjured. Dr. Thatcher wasn't reciprocating my advances.

His condo was messy, filled with empty grocery bags and protein bars. Post-apocalyptic. He looked uncomfortable, distant.

"What's this about?" he asked, his tone cautious.

"Oh, um, okay," I stumbled, trying to regain my composure. "So—"

"Wait. If this is going to be self-incriminating, Cindy, I don't want to hear it."

His words cut through the haze. Was this how he viewed me? A liability?

TOO MUCH

I pushed forward, "Okay, but, is it just me, or is there, like, a thing between us?"

"Oh, Cindy. No." He stepped back, hands raised. "I'm sorry, but we absolutely can't. There absolutely can't be anything unprofessional between us. I'm an attending, and you're a resident."

The rejection stung, but I persisted. We engaged in a tense exchange, with me desperately seeking validation and him firmly rebuffing my advances. It was a humiliating dance of shameless desires and harsh realities.

Defeated, I returned to the condo, the silence amplified by Paul's indifference. The office door still shut. The night had been a disaster, a stark reminder of the growing chasm in my marriage and the emptiness within myself.

The unspoken truth of that night lingered between Dr. Thatcher and me, a silent testament to a reckless impulse and a painful rejection. The lies in my marriage continued to fester, leaving me yearning for something more, something real.

CHAPTER 12

Leis

June 2021, Hawaii

Time was evaporating. Dr. Thatcher took a permanent position at another hospital—news that brought a mix of relief and disappointment. Relief that the awkward encounters would cease, but disappointment that the what-ifs would remain unresolved. My embarrassing misstep, my fleeting hope for a connection outside my troubled marriage, would simply fade into the background noise of life.

Meanwhile, Paul's graduation loomed large, a stark reminder of the diverging paths our lives were taking. He, a convicted felon, was on the cusp of becoming an attending, while I, four years into residency, still grappled with uncertainty and the looming threat of dismissal. The weight of our disparate situations pressed down on me, fueling my resentment and amplifying the loneliness that had settled deep within my bones.

Because of Covid, his graduation ceremony was tucked away in a small room at his training hospital. Just a few people were allowed to attend.

Paul's program had him wearing a Hawaiian drape over his suit. He was one of two white people graduating. Maybe that's why he felt like such an outcast.

Growing up in the Hawaiian melting pot, I didn't focus on what a person "was."

But this question came at me every day in med school and residency: "What are you?"

It became routine to explain that I am "hapa,"—being from Hawaii is different than being Kānaka Maoli, Native Hawaiian

Twenty years later, Hawaii felt so different, and I couldn't help but empathize with Paul—*the haole outsider*. He must have felt so alone, watching his classmates laugh, hug their families and exchange leis.

As his wife, I forgot to bring him a lei…I forgot. I didn't have a lei for my husband on his big graduation day. I failed him. I decided it would be the last time.

Paul had spent months looking for a hospitalist job on the island. But they all required two to three years of experience. He was able to find a two-month locum job on Kauai, which he accepted. He'd be moving in three weeks. The plan was for me to finish out my last year of residency. Then live together again.

The graduation ceremony ended, and a heavy silence settled between as we made our way home. The artificial cheer of the event had evaporated, leaving only the unspoken tension that had been simmering beneath the surface for months. I knew this was the moment. Taking a deep breath, I turned to Paul. "Paul, I'm really proud of you," I said, and I meant it.

"Thank you, Cindy." Paul's fierce determination and resilience reminded me that a person could go to hell and back and still come out ahead.

"I'm sorry you couldn't find a job here."

"I tried."

"Paul," I said, taking a deep breath, "We need to get a divorce."

"Is there someone else?" he asked, almost automatically.

"What? No."

"Who is it?" He came towards me.

I stepped back, the renovated walls of the condo caving in on me. This all felt so familiar, so scary.

Truthfully, I *wished* one of us was cheating. It would have made things easier.

"This hasn't been working for a long time, Paul. You know that. You've been sleeping in the other room. We don't have sex. We don't treat each other like we're married."

Paul walked over to the canvas wedding photo I ordered just after our wedding. He'd always hated it but never told me why. He ripped it off the wall, slammed it across his knee, breaking the cheap wooden frame in half, then ripped the canvas to shreds, like a monster.

"What the fuck are you doing?"

TOO MUCH

He yelled and sent the mess sailing across the living room.

We watched the canvas float to the floor, and then Paul fell onto the couch with his head in his hands.

"I promise there's nobody else," I pleaded. Afraid he was going to lunge at me. Afraid he would snap, worse than either of us ever have before.

"It doesn't make any sense, then. If there's nobody else, then what the fuck is the problem? I have a job now. I graduated. We did it. And now you want to divorce me?"

Paul looked up at me, defeated. Crushed. I knew he still loved me. And I loved him. But no matter how much loved each other. It wasn't enough.

I looked at him with a million thoughts swirling in my head. Didn't he feel the distance between us? A divorce made all the sense in the world. Paul would be fine on his own now. I supported him, I had done my penance for helping him break his marriage vows, and now we could go our separate ways. This wasn't the fairytale ending I once envisioned, filled with romantic getaways and Valentine's roses—a total Ken and Barbie cliché. But as my father once told me, all good things must come to pass.

At least this way, we could finally be free.

I couldn't muster the strength to say any of that out loud. Instead, I quietly picked up the tattered pieces of canvas and splintered bits of wood off the floor.

Leis

* * *

July 2021, Main Hospital, Hawaii

As a way of showing my appreciation for his mentorship, I updated Major Ernst about my progress in residency. But I didn't share details about Paul, our divorce.

"Did you receive the investigation findings?" he asked.

I went home and checked my emails—I missed the reply to my request for the investigation findings in accordance with the Freedom of Information Act…the email said I had to sign another form and file another request with another office. Seemed easy enough, so I did.

* * *

July 2021, Waikiki

Hawaii Place was Suzy's favorite. We reserved the private dining room for her graduation. I arrived early in a frilly pink dress, designer heels, and a fresh blowout. I delivered a speech that was more of a roast than a heartfelt farewell.

When the party died down, I drunkenly stumbled to the bustling streets of Waikiki and called Dr. Thatcher, wondering if maybe he could give me a ride. I regretted it as soon as it went to voicemail. How embarrassing. *Who had I bothered to dress up for? What a waste.*

I ordered a rideshare and slipped into the back, utterly disappointed. Even though people laughed at my jokes, complimented my dress, called me pretty, I didn't feel wanted, accepted, or valued. I checked Paul's location from my phone. He wasn't home. It was midnight.

"How's your night going?" the driver asked. He glanced at me through his rearview mirror, his eyes seeming to linger on my lips.

"It's fine," I said.

"You look sad." His dark mysterious eyes met mine.

"I'm not sad." I cracked a smile and looked out the window.

"Wanna to grab a drink?"

I sat there and rubbed the leather on my designer clutch. I could barely see his entire face but caught his gaze again. "Sure."

"Okay, I'll cancel the ride."

And just like that, I was being whisked away. As we drove through the neon-lit streets, I stole some glances, his enigmatic smile both comforting and creepy.

"Call me Jay," he said.

After bar-hopping without successfully getting a drink due to over-whelming crowds, Jay and I found ourselves buying small bottles of liquor, chips, and roll-up sandwiches at a convenience store. Cradling our loot and laughing, we checked into a lurky hotel across the street.

The next morning, Jay dropped me off in front of my condo, and

Leis

I stumbled in, forgetting that Paul existed. I honestly relished the thought that I had gone "missing."

Paul popped out from beneath the white sheets in the main bedroom, where he hadn't slept once since moving back in. "Where the fuck have you been all night?" he yelled.

"What?"

"I asked, where were you?"

"At a friends'."

"At a friend's? Yeah, fucking right."

"What does it matter? We're getting divorced," I reminded him.

"Yeah, fucking right we are."

I nestled up to him and wrapped my arms around his sweaty belly, but he pushed me away. I retreated to the bathroom and examined my smudged make-up in the mirror. Even though Paul was angry, and had good reason to be, I still hoped he'd come in to see me.

I took off my clothes and stood in the steaming hotness of my mess. When he didn't come in, I stepped into the shower and attempted to wash all the whore-ness and shame and blame off myself. I didn't actually want Jay, or a random hook-up. I wanted a world in which my husband loved me, and we could stay together.

I scrubbed my skin raw, desperate to erase the night's events, but the memories clung to me like the lingering scent of Jay's cologne. I thought about the note Paul wrote me when he gave me a watch for my birthday:

> For the good times, the bad times, and only what time will tell.

It was obvious now that he would never promise me a life of everlasting love. Our wedding day made that perfectly clear. And yet, I pursued it, clinging to a dying relationship, until it finally crumbled to dust.

I pursued unavailable men and toxic romance, stuck in a cycle of overwhelming affection followed by abrupt withdrawal. This was not love; it was trauma bonding and toxic narcissism.

When I was interviewing for residency, one of the program directors told me, "I only pick people with baggage, because they have something to prove, because they are willing to do whatever it takes." He saw my desperation.

Maybe this mentality was the problem. It allowed medical programs to abuse students seeking validation, working them to the bone. All I had done was deprive myself of a life worth living, reinforcing the emptiness inside. I had subjected myself to humiliation, sleep deprivation, starvation, sexual harassment, and impossible ideals, neglecting myself and buying into the idea that I needed to change everything about myself to succeed.

I felt like a puppet in a toxic environment. And yet, I still couldn't walk away. I was addicted.

Leis

* * *

July 2021, Main Hospital, Hawaii

Flap surgeries were long and complex, a test of my skills and endurance as a fourth-year resident on probation. The pressure to perform flawlessly was intense, especially under the watchful eyes of Dr. Pratt and the notoriously critical Dr. Bates. After a grueling 26-hour surgery, I made the mistake of missing my BLS recertification class.

On Monday, Dr. Bates called me to his office. "We're extending your probation," he said. "You can't go to Vista Hospital. This BLS lapse is unacceptable."

I had no defense. It was my fault. I failed again. With a heavy heart, I signed the probation paperwork, feeling like I was signing my life away.

* * *

July 2021, Oahu Beach Park

Two weeks later, I was invited to a BBQ. An excuse for incoming interns and jaded senior residents to get sloshed on the beach. Jennifer insisted there would be *hot guys*—I hadn't broken the news to her about Paul and I breaking up, yet.

The sun was beating down on the sand, littered with empty beer cans, red cups, pizza boxes. Everyone was wasted. There had to be almost 100 people raging in the middle of broad daylight. Normally, I'd be into it. But with the news that I was going to be stuck at Main for who knows how long—I knew that drinking wouldn't fix things. Neither would any "hot guy"—not that I was ready for it.

Jen was hammered, wearing a revealing white sundress, her curly hair tossing in the wind as she jiggled around. She threw her arm around me. Surprised me with, "Hey—did you hear about this whole cheating scandal in ENT?"

"What?" I pretended to have no idea what she was talking about.

"Yeah—one of the ortho attendings was talking about it to the residents in the OR—"

"How—I mean which ortho resident are you talking to?" I caught myself mid-sentence and smirked.

"Nobody." Her eyes sparkled with drunken mischief, and a wide grin spread across her face.

"Who is he?" I took a deep breath, trying to maintain composure.

"Nobody, I swear!" She giggled and looked over at a group of guys playing cornhole.

"Oh my gosh—crazy. I would never date a surgeon."

"Never say never! Wait—so what is this drama? What's happening?"

"Yeah, Cindy, tell us everything," Gabi said, dressed in her slinky hot pink one piece.

I paused, my throat tightening as I struggled to find the right words. "I...we're not supposed to talk about it," I mumbled. I motioned to Jen's drink, taking a long sip.

"Dude—that's so f*cken crazy—I heard someone snitched. Like who would do that?" Gabi leaned forward, her eyes widening with curiosity. She rested her chin on her hand, her long, painted nails tapping against her cheek.

"Oh—crazy. Yeah. I don't know."

"I know, right?" Jennifer cooed, her speech slightly slurred. "Like, what kind of person snitches like that?"

"It's...complicated," I muttered, averting my eyes and taking a sip of my drink.

"Okay, well. Whatever—um. Let's play corn hole! Do you want a shot first?"

"Yes. Shots."

I glanced at the group of guys playing cornhole—Steve, Tony, and all the other boys from ENT—laughing, drinking, as if they didn't have a care in the world. A pang of jealousy hit me, and I quickly looked away, hoping no one noticed the fleeting expression of pain on my face. I went home and checked on the FOIA request. Still nothing.

CHAPTER 13

Shots

August 2021, Kona, Hawaii

Every summer, the program mandated a self-funded ENT "Rezzy Retreat" on one of the Hawaiian Islands. The team-building usually devolved into heavy drinking and oversharing. During my second year, I was labeled the "Karen" of the group after taking the keys from a drunken Adam who wanted to off-road the rental car on private property. Third year was more enjoyable, filled with drinking games and impersonations, a temporary escape from the pressures of residency.

This year, I should have been a chief resident, but due to my probation, I was still a "subordinate." Dr. Bates and Steve enlisted my help to plan the retreat in Kona. We hiked, snorkeled, and drank by the pool. After dusk, the drinking intensified.

As the night wore on, conversations turned to politics and religion. Jeff's drunken rant about the war in Afghanistan triggered my social anxiety. Tony tried to explain the situation, but I feigned ignorance, retreating into my "Drunk Barbie" persona. I couldn't help but think of Paul, how he had suffered in silence after his deployments.

After Steve went to bed, Tony and I continued drinking whiskey shots in the Jacuzzi. He drunkenly said I had made "noticeable differences" and was more fun to work with, then hinted at a secret he wanted to share, but never did. Later, Tony and I joined Maria for a sunrise hike up Mauna Kea.

We passed out in the car. When I opened my eyes, Tony was snuggled up against my shoulder, holding my hand in the backseat. I was so confused. I dropped his hand, terrified that Maria would see. Tony and I never talked about any of it. The handholding. The hot tub.

Tony never ended up revealing his secret, if there even was one. I can't help but think that if he had, things might have turned out differently. Instead, an awkward tension developed between us, a silent reminder of unsaid words and missed opportunities.

* * *

September 2021, Vista Hospital, Hawaii

Thankfully, the period after the retreat was quiet and productive. A summons came down from Dr. Pratt and Dr. Bates a few weeks later. I was so conditioned to be disappointed that I flinched whenever I was called to their office. This time, though, it was good news.

"Cindy, the CCC met and agreed to remove you from probationary status. We will be sending you to Vista Hospital for your away rotation in two weeks. It's short notice, but you need to submit proof of vaccinations," Dr. Bates said.

Tony's words about noticeable differences rang in my head. Maybe he wasn't just drunk and full of shit. Even though I never learned his secret, I was hugely relieved.

Two weeks later, I met Jennifer in the cafeteria of Vista Hospital. She'd already been there for a few weeks on OBGYN rotations and was eager to share her insights.

"Welcome to the Promised Land!" she squealed, adding tomatoes and a couple of mangoes to her basket. "They have the best fruits and vegetables. You know we get a $30 a day stipend here, right?"

Jennifer was a force of nature, her enthusiasm infectious. She had a knack for finding the bright side of any situation, a quality I desperately needed in my life.

"Ooh, bottled Starbucks," I said, allowing myself to get excited. The little things felt monumental after the constant stress at Main Hospital.

"Oh, yeah, girl, stock up! Literally, you can grocery shop here, it's amazing. But remember, just $30 a day."

"Seriously?" I asked, trying to hide my shock. "That's amazing! I'm used to surviving off vending machine snacks and the occasional freebie from patients."

Jennifer laughed. "Girl, you need to treat yourself! This is Vista, not Main. We actually get to live a little here."

Just $30 a day? This was an unheard-of perk, and every cent of it seemed like a dream come true. We walked down the hall to the physician's lounge, and Jennifer punched her key code into the door. A TV blared the news, rehashing the situation in Afghanistan, and a row of computers faced the indoor garden courtyard. A handful of our co-residents took up most of the seats. We squeezed into the last two empty spots.

"Cindy?"

I looked over at the guy wearing thick black glasses. He had brown freckles and light tan skin. His mask was tied around the back of his neck, pulled below his chin. He flashed a quirky smile at me and waved.

I vaguely remembered that his name was Brad, or maybe Chad. We'd met a while ago at one of those drunk karaoke intern nights. He was probably one of the chief residents now, like I should've been. I couldn't believe he remembered me.

Once he turned back to his computer, I leaned over to Jennifer and whispered, "Hey, that's one of the Ortho chiefs, right... Bradley?"

She laughed. "Yeah, Bradley Brown. He goes by Brad. He's a total sweetheart. And single, by the way." She winked, her eyes sparkling with mischief.

Bradley got up to leave, but not before we looked at one another once more. A spark of curiosity ignited within me.

I took a long sip of my bottled Starbucks. "Is he, like, married now or something?"

"He had a bad break-up recently. Why? You interested?"

"Oh, just wondering. I figure most surgical chiefs are married by now. That's all."

"Uh-huh, right," she teased, her smile was a welcome distraction from my anxiety.

Something at this hospital felt so different. The hallways seemed brighter; the people friendlier. I didn't hear whispers wherever I went or laughter behind my back. There were no huddles, no cliques. And when I walked up to a nurse to introduce myself, she said, "Welcome, we are so happy to have you here."

For the first time in a long while, I believed it.

* * *

October 2021, The Promised Land, Hawaii

Overall, my rotation was going well. No incidents, reports, or arguments. The Promised Land was night-and-day compared to Main Hospital. I felt like an entirely different person. I lost weight. I was drinking water, eating healthier, and exercising. I looked and felt happier.

And I kept bumping into Bradley Brown.

We'd casually strike up conversations, our shared love for the ocean creating an easy rapport. One day, he showed me a picture of a sailboat on his phone.

"I was thinking of buying this boat if I end up in San Francisco for fellowship. Check it out," his eyes sparkling. "Someday I want to sail around the world."

"No way, I want to sail around the world someday, too!" I squealed, my own dreams taking flight. "But to SCUBA dive and save animals. I could make a documentary for *National Geographic* about oil spills. It's a vibe."

A surprised smile spread across his face. "Wait, I used to work for them. We did shark adventures."

"Get out! I love sharks! My ex and I went looking for hammerheads once in Japan, and another time in Maui!"

"No way. I love sharks too. I love all the sea animals. We should go SCUBA diving sometime. Like with a friend group," he said, his voice trailing off, a hint of something more than friendship in his eyes.

* * *

January 2017, Japan

During our last year of med school, Paul and I eclipsed reality in Okinawa to study Neurology. It was a heavenly month filled with soba noodles, fresh sushi, and the most tropical beaches, rich with vibrant corals. We spent the weekends scuba diving. The cool ocean breeze whipped through my hair as we stood on the deck of the boat, anticipation thrumming through us.

We were about to embark on a bucket-list adventure: diving with schools of hammerhead sharks. It was a long weekend so we hopped to another island, just for these hammerheads. Met American doctors on the trip, who joked that we should do anything but medicine.

Paul and I had a special underwater camera and tried to snap pics. Identifying little animals and clownfish, seeing what we could possibly frame at home—became a fun vacation hobby. As we descended, a school of majestic creatures materialized from the deep blue. Their sleek bodies effortlessly gliding along, their wide-set eyes scanning the water with eerie intelligence.

On our dives together, I felt a profound connection to Paul, a shared sense of wonder and excitement. When we resurfaced, safe and sound, we were laughing. Happy. A shared moment of pure joy turned into a memory that would later haunt me with its bittersweet reminder of what was lost. Blurry photographs snapped underwater, never to be framed.

* * *

October 2021, Kaka'ako, Hawaii

The text from Brad about a mutual patient arrived unexpectedly. My heart fluttered as I saved his contact. A few days later, over drinks with Gracie, my excitement spilled out.

"I think there could be a thing between us," I confessed, a nervous thrill in my voice. "He's single. It's probably nothing, but…should we…invite him out?"

Gracie, ever the voice of reason, raised an eyebrow. "Cindy. You're getting divorced!"

But the allure of possibility was too strong.

"Oh, come on. Let's have a drink with him. Please?" I pleaded, suddenly wishing Jennifer, with her fearless spirit, was here instead.

"I highly doubt he'll come, but okay, text him," Gracie conceded, her tone laced with skepticism.

My fingers flew across the screen, anticipation buzzing in my veins. To my surprise, Brad's reply came almost instantly:

> Sure. Where you guys at?

"Oh. Em. Gee. He says he'll come!" I squealed, barely containing my excitement.

Gracie's eyes widened. "Seriously?"

But then another text followed:

> I'll bring my date if that's okay.

My stomach plummeted. "Oh, my gosh, he's bringing a chick." A wave of disappointment washed over me. "Do you think it's his ex? I peeked at her Insta...she's so pretty!"

"This is super weird, Cindy," Gracie muttered, her disapproval evident.

"What? I did it from my stalker account—"

"Your stalker account?!"

TOO MUCH

"Yeah, doesn't everyone have one?"

Gracie rolled her eyes and laughed. We headed to Drink Date, a trendy bar in town, and ordered drinks. Shared an appetizer and caught up on her life—she was in a new marketing job that allowed her to work from home. We fantasized about traveling to Dubai someday. The night was pulsing, a vibrant backdrop of murals behind us, thumping bass, and laughter.

I almost forgot Brad was coming and then he popped up with not one, but *two* women, one of whom was an ICU nurse from Vista. The initial awkwardness gave way to a strange camaraderie fueled by endless rounds of shots. Brad's foot brushed against my ankle under the table, sending a jolt of electricity through me. But the more I drank, the more blurred the lines became.

The night ended in a haze of alcohol-induced oblivion. I remember flashes: Brad paying the bill, suggesting sushi sometime, and Gracie's scolding as we stumbled home.

"Cindy, that was so bad!" she hissed. "You were hitting on him in front of his dates! Asking them to take you back for a foursome. Oh my gosh, you are so predictably unpredictable! Also, Cindy—you know Brad is a f*ckboy right!"

"What's that—"

"Seriously? You don't know what a f*ckboy is!? Oh my gosh. Cindy. You need to treat him like a f*ckboy. All guys like this—treat them like f*ckboys. Trust me."

Shots

"Ugh, okay, I'll Google it."

I winced, the shame of my drunken behavior washing over me. I knew it was wrong to flirt with Brad in front of his dates, but a part of me clung to the hope that he reciprocated my feelings. The night had been a chaotic mix of emotions, leaving me with more questions than answers. Brad didn't seem like a f*ckboy at all, but maybe she was right. I made mistakes with Paul in the past—and Brad did show up with two dates.

Once again, I was trying to ignore all the red flags. How could I resist? Maybe I just loved toxic too much.

* * *

October 2021, The Promised Land

I looked around the OR, a smile tugging at my lips. An all-female team—a rare sight.

The anesthesiologist grinned. "Ladies, it's a girls' OR today!"

A chorus of laughter filled the room.

"Hey, Cindy," a nurse called out, "did you do anything fun this weekend?"

"Just chilled at home," I replied, omitting the part about grappling with social anxiety and skipping a gathering.

"Same here," another nurse chimed in. "Sometimes, a quiet weekend is just what the doctor ordered."

The Promised Land felt like a breath of fresh air compared to Main Hospital. The atmosphere was more relaxed, the conversations more open. The attending surgeon, Dr. Jai, was a no-nonsense woman with a warm smile. As she skillfully navigated the sinus surgery, she shared a personal anecdote.

"I got married the day before an in-service practice test in med school," she chuckled. "The score didn't even count, but they wouldn't let me skip it. I filled in random bubbles and left."

A ripple of laughter went through the room.

"Do you want kids?" she asked me suddenly.

"Um, I actually just filed for divorce," I stammered, caught off guard.

"Good for you," she said simply.

"Thanks," I replied, surprised by her lack of judgment.

"Have you thought about freezing your eggs?" she continued. "We did that a few years ago."

The question lingered for a moment as I watched her blitz bone chips and suction blood. It was a topic I had considered, a way to preserve a future I wasn't sure I wanted.

"Yeah, I might look into it," I hesitated.

This casual conversation about such a personal topic was a revelation. It was a stark contrast to the forced therapy sessions and superficial interactions I'd endured at Main Hospital. Here, I felt a sense of camaraderie, a shared understanding among women navigating the challenges of medicine and life.

"Hang in there," Dr. Jai said, without taking her eyes of the screen. "The best thing you can do in residency, and in life, is to be undeniably good when you feel like the odds are against you."

Her words resonated deeply. It was the first time someone in a position of authority had encouraged me to strive for excellence, not just survival.

* * *

November 2021, Hawaii

Six weeks at The Promised Land flew by, and I was devastated to be returning to Main Hospital. My reentry happened during another Friday Academics session, except Dr. Bates had asked that all ten residents come in an hour early. A familiar knot tightened in my stomach.

"I wanted you all here today for this news," Dr. Bates announced, his voice grave. "The National Board of Otolaryngology contacted us last week to notify us that we are being investigated for allegations of cheating on the annual in-service exam. They will be flying out next week to conduct interviews with all of the residents and most of the staff."

The room fell silent, the air thick with tension. How could this be happening as soon as I returned to Main like I was cursed? I avoided eye contact, but I could feel the accusing stares of my colleagues. Jeff, Tony, Nick—their eyes bore into me, as if I were the sole culprit. Will, a new resident, shifted uncomfortably beside me, his grip tightening on his phone.

"Materials that were recently provided." Who could have provided them? The emails I sent were a year old. This couldn't be my doing.

A flicker of hope ignited within me. Did I finally have an ally in this twisted game?

CHAPTER 14

Years

November 2021, Main Hospital, Hawaii

"Who would say something?" Nick whispered in the hushed resident room.

Steve, ever the optimist, offered a nervous chuckle. "Maybe it was that Facebook post? You know, the one where we were all bragging about being number one."

Tony burst in, his face a mask of fury. "Can someone put in a transfer order for me?" he snarled, slamming his hand on the desk. "These nurses are useless."

Nick jumped to his feet. "Sure, Tony. What's the problem?"

"My patient's on the floor, but the system still shows them in recovery. No one can pull their meds. It's been fucking hours!" Tony's voice echoed with barely contained rage.

Nick quickly logged into the system. "No problem, I'll get it done."

Tony slumped back in his chair, muttering curses under his breath.

Steve, sensing the growing unease, tried to lighten the mood. "Hey, at least we don't have to deal with insurance companies here like they do at Vista," he said, a forced smile on his face. "Remember those endless approval calls, Nick?"

Nick nodded grimly. "Yeah, that was a pain."

The conversation inevitably shifted to the investigation, and Steve's bravado wavered. "Honestly, guys, I don't think we have anything to worry about," he said, his voice tinged with doubt. "They're just doing their job. We didn't do anything wrong."

But his words did little to quell the anxiety that had settled over the room. Nick, usually the quietest of the group, broke the silence. "Do you think we need a lawyer?"

All eyes turned to me.

* * *

December 2021, Main Hospital, Hawaii

It felt good. The spark of recognition. The air crackled between us. Brad locked his gaze on me and I couldn't stop staring. Those extra seconds of eye contact told me that I. Was. Not. Crazy. To feel those vibes. To think that there was—and maybe still could be—something between us. I had to keep moving along with the team, but, after we passed each other, I could feel him staring at my back. Or at least—I hoped it.

Hours later, decked out in my surgical gear, I saw him again outside the OR.

"Whoa, what's with the fancy get-up?" he asked, a playful grin spreading across his face.

"Just gotta pee," realizing how ridiculous I must look with my headlight and loupes.

He chuckled, blocking my path. "Nice."

I sidestepped him, my heart pounding. "Well, have a good day!"

After the case, my phone lit up with a barrage of texts from Brad.

> Hey it was so great seeing you! I realized we never went on that sushi date?!! We should go sometime!

I screenshotted the texts and fired them off to my friends, a giddy feeling bubbling up inside me.

> Does Thursday work for you? I replied, my fingers trembling slightly.

> Yes. Let's make a date.

Never realized? How does someone not ever realize they didn't go on a date? Sounded a bit clueless and like a total f*ckboy excuse but regardless, the entire situation sent a thrill through me. Maybe this could be something.

Thursday night found us at The Hibiscus Hideaway, surrounded by the soft glow of candlelight and the sweet scent of orchids. Brad's eyes sparkled as he asked, "Have you ever dated another doctor?"

"Well, my husband—I mean, ex," I stumbled over the word, still adjusting to my new reality.

"No," he replied, his gaze never leaving mine. "How's that going? I'm sorry, by the way."

"The paperwork isn't finalized yet," I said, a bittersweet smile touching my lips. "But I'm happier than I've been in years. I feel...free."

He nodded, a thoughtful look on his face. "That's good to hear."

We talked for hours that night, sharing our dreams and fears. He told me about his aspirations in aerospace medicine, his passion for space exploration. I confessed my uncertainties about the future, my longing for a fresh start.

As we walked back to my place, the warm Waikiki night air filled with the distant sound of waves crashing against the shore, Brad pulled down my mask and kissed me. The unexpectedness of it made us both laugh.

"What's so funny?" I asked, breathless.

"I don't know! We're kissing in the middle of Waikiki!"

In that moment, all my doubts and insecurities melted away. Maybe this *was* real. Maybe Brad was the fresh start I had been craving. But deep down, a nagging fear lingered. Was I good enough for him? Did I deserve happiness?

* * *

Years

December 2021, Main Hospital, Hawaii

As the investigation loomed, a mix of paranoia and relief waxed and waned. On one hand, it was kind of thrilling having a secret—on the other, it was frightening to wonder when everyone would figure out it was me. Dr. Bates assured us the hospital's attorney would be present, but memories of Paul's legal battles resurfaced. Government-assigned attorneys, we were warned, protected the government, not the individual.

The morning of the interviews, I found myself in a nondescript building on another base, my heart pounding against my starched uniform. After an eternity of getting lost, I finally signed in. Only Dr. Pratt and Dr. Bates were ahead of me.

Spotting the attorney, I felt compelled to introduce myself. "How long have you been doing this?" I asked, attempting small talk.

"Over twenty years," she mumbled, eyes glued to her phone. "But I just got this position three months ago."

Before I could probe further, an older gentleman appeared. "Captain Neighbors?"

"Yes, sir." I rose, the attorney trailing behind.

As we reached the conference room, I turned to the gentleman. "Does she have to join? Is it mandatory?"

"No, if you don't want her to."

I looked at the attorney, her eyes narrowed in annoyance. "I'd prefer to do the interview alone, please."

She huffed and retreated to the waiting room. Inside the conference room, five interviewers sat in a circle, their faces a mixture of curiosity and concern.

"Cindy, thank you for doing what you did," one began. "We know it wasn't easy. You did the right thing."

I blinked back tears, surprised by their gratitude.

"May I ask...why did you do it?"

I hesitated, then spoke from the heart. "The cheating was wrong. I was tired of the toxic culture it fostered. When I reported it to Dr. Pratt and nothing happened, I felt like the whole system was a sham."

I paused, remembering Paul's induction into the Gold Humanism Honor Society in medical school. An honor I never achieved, despite my dedication to patient care. It was Paul who had always encouraged me to stand up for what was right, even when it was difficult.

"I didn't expose the cheating to hurt anyone," I continued. "I did it hoping to make things better. But I'm not sure it will."

A heavy silence fell over the room. I felt the familiar sting of shame, the fear that I had betrayed my colleagues. But then I remembered why I had done it.

"This cheating is unfair to patients," I said, my voice growing stronger.

"We're supposed to be trustworthy healers, not frauds who cut corners. Our board certification should mean something."

I looked at each interviewer in turn, their faces impassive. Did they understand? Did they care?

"The culture of medicine needs to change," I continued. "Why are we so desperate to prove ourselves that we're willing to sacrifice our integrity? We need to create a system where people can thrive without compromising their values."

Silence. Had I gone too far? Had I doomed my career? As I left the conference room, a wave of exhaustion washed over me. I had done what I believed was right, but the consequences were still uncertain. I called Paul, needing the reassurance of a familiar voice, the comfort of a shared secret.

"I did it," I whispered into the phone. "I told them everything."

There was a long pause on the other end of the line. "I'm proud of you, Cindy," Paul said finally. "You did the right thing."

His words were a lifeline, a reminder that even in the darkest of times, there was still hope for a brighter future.

* * *

December 2021, Main Hospital, Hawaii

Dr. Bates called all of the residents into the mahogany table conference room. These meetings were becoming eerily routine. Most of the attendings were present, their faces grim. The screen projector was lit up, ready to drop some big news.

"So, do we know the outcome of the NBO investigation?" Tony asked, his voice laced with a nervous energy that belied his usual bravado.

I squirmed, a knot tightening in my stomach. This was it.

"Thank you, everyone, for being here today," Dr. Bates began, his voice strained. He avoided eye contact, fumbling with the projector remote. "I'm afraid I have some bad news. In a gesture of full transparency, I want to show you the letter we received."

The wall in front of us lit up with a letterhead from the NCRA.

"The NCRA gave us ten citations this year," Dr. Bates announced, he lowered his voice. "Including citations for gender discrimination, harassment, performing non-physician duties, and not recognizing the signs of substance disorder."

A stunned silence fell over the room. I glanced at Tony, his face pale. He met my gaze, a flicker of fear in his eyes.

"This is based on the surveys you all filled out a couple of months ago," Dr. Pratt interjected, her voice sharp. "In order for the program to get cited, the results have to be analyzed and reviewed by Main Hospital command. The NCRA wants a typed report from us. They don't take citations lightly."

"What do you mean, 'reviewed'?" Jeff asked, his voice laced with suspicion. "What's to review?"

Dr. Bates cleared his throat, his eyes darting around the room. "Dr. Pratt and I plan to meet with each year's residents in small groups to discuss how we can improve the program. It will help us write a response letter to the NCRA."

"We'll also be sending out more surveys," Dr. Pratt added. "We want to gather more information on these allegations and complaints."

Tony leaned forward, his voice low and urgent. "For starters, we have a severe staffing shortage. We're constantly doing the work of nurses and techs. It's impacting our training."

Dr. Bates nodded slowly, his face etched with worry. "We hear you, Tony. We're working on addressing the staffing issue."

Tony and I exchanged a knowing glance. Was this the moment we'd been waiting for? Was the program finally going to be held accountable?

"Just because something's been done a certain way for a long time doesn't make it right," Steve spoke up, his voice surprisingly firm.

Hope hit me like a sunrise. Maybe I wasn't alone in this fight. Maybe there were others who wanted to see real change.

"Can't we go to someone higher up and explain the situation?" Tony suggested, his voice filled with a newfound determination. "Our accreditation is at stake."

Dr. Pratt's expression hardened. "We've already been in contact with higher command," she said, her tone clipped." They're aware of the situation."

Dr. Bates sighed, his shoulders slumping. "I've decided to step down as program director."

The room erupted in whispers and gasps. I stared at Dr. Bates, a mix of emotions swirling within me. Was this a victory? Or just another twist in the never-ending saga of the Main Hospital ENT program?

As the meeting adjourned, Tony caught my eye and gave me a subtle nod. *What if Tony wanted the same thing as me? What if I wasn't as crazy as I thought? Or even if I was crazy…maybe there was still a chance that I could graduate from this program.*

Who cares if I was just barely hanging on by a thread—anything to graduate.

Even if I was scathed. Maybe everything could work out.

CHAPTER 15

Friends

December 2021, Hawaii

It was just before New Year's Eve, my birthday.

Steve had me scheduled for two days of overbooked clinics in between ER doctors calling for various consults. Holidays were the season for bar brawls and black eyes, but, alas, actual cases with indications for surgeries weren't presenting, and the residents were all starving to scrub in on traumas.

Dr. Bates once interrogated me. "If you had to save a guy, and he was bleeding out in Iraq from his carotid, could you do it?"

I struggled to frame my answer... "I don't know...?" Then I ran back to Will and Steve to make sure I'd gotten it right, and they laughed.

"Uh, it depends on a lot of circumstances. What else is happening? Who else is there?" Steve said. "Chances are if someone is bleeding out from their carotid, no, unless you have an OR...good luck."

That's what I'd suspected, but Dr. Bates made it seem like I had to answer "yes." After five years at a hospital that hadn't taught much head and neck trauma, I was reassured yet disturbed to find out that there were situations where I would be powerless. Instead, I was self-teaching how to inject Botox and filler thanks to my work besties after hours and how to game the broken system.

"Hey, why do you guys think Dr. Bates is stepping down early?" I asked.

"It's not early. It's been five years," Steve said.

"But he has six months left before he's supposed to step down," Tony said.

"Well, he says he wants to move back to the mainland for his wife or something. I think they want to have another kid."

"That doesn't really make sense, Steve," I said.

"Aren't you happy about it?" Steve asked.

"Why? I'm fine with him. I mean, he's the one who seems to think I have a problem, but I'm fine." I insisted.

"Okay…" Steve said.

Tony looked pensive. "Dude. Do you think it's about the cheating thing or the complications?"

"What complications?" I asked.

"You know—" Tony gave me a look, like I *knew*.

"No," Steve interrupted, "that kind of stuff happens."

Friends

Although Will, Steve, and Tony seemed like possible allies, they weren't completely trustworthy. With the complaints against Main Hospital, I wondered whether they, too, were fed up with not getting to operate enough or experience a wide variety of surgical cases.

We claimed to be number one on Facebook, but I questioned if it was true. After returning from The Promised Land, I was back to binge drinking and stress eating. The bougie food truck, Chunky Burgers and Fries—oversized juicy burgers with extra-greasy fries drizzled in special sauce and bacon bits—beckoned my soul.

As I sped away from Main Hospital on a rare break, I tossed my phone and watched it bounce off the leather seat next to my worn-out, taped-up pager. They both ricocheted to the floor, haphazardly piled up with dirty scrubs and scribbled patient notes. The Kaka'ako air was warm and sticky on my face. The burger I'd been craving suddenly didn't seem like such a good idea for my digestive tract, but who was I kidding? I wasn't eating for nutrition. I wanted to eat my feelings.

Just as I got my meal and was busy numbing out in the front seat of my car, an email dropped.

From: noreply@anonymousemailservers.com
Subject: residency exam cheating
The exam cheating is real, rampant, and historic especially it being actively encouraged by prior program directors. Unless you expose this problem into the spotlight with help from media, these things will only get buried and you will face backlash for the rest of your military career. Look out

for yourself because no one in the military will ever look out for you.

I sat up in my seat, burger forgotten. My hands shaking. Was this a message of support? Although it was anonymous, it seemed like a sudden lifeline. The program might have been a fraud, but I realized that I was, too.

A snitch and a fraud. I had reported the program and then acted maybe even more surprised than anyone when NBO showed up. An Academy Award-worthy performance, maybe.

Or maybe not.

The larger ramifications of what might happen next unspooled in my mind. Military otolaryngologists have arguably contributed a great deal to the field of Otolaryngology. If the program tanked, my actions could have a greater impact than I imagined.

Up to this point, most people just chalked me up as the "bitchy one," or the woman looking out for herself. Then I became something more problematic, more dangerous.

A whistleblower…? I quickly looked up the definition. I know, it's ridiculous. Looking up the definition of something I did, after doing it. But what else was I supposed to do?

Did I do something…wrong? Could I be a female Ed Snow…?! What if I got arrested? Exported. Oh god. It wasn't about just speaking *my* truth. I was fighting for *the* truth. I wasn't alone. I was horrified.

Friends

This *anonymous email supporter* seemed to know something. The other people lodging complaints knew, too. The message heralded a very real and immediate threat to my job, my case against Main Hospital, my livelihood, my future, and perhaps even my life.

It all sounds so dramatic, but in a sick, cynical way…what some may consider a threat sparked a little hope.

Some random person cared. Somewhere.

The question was who?

And more importantly—why?

* * *

January 2022, Main Hospital, Hawaii

After the holidays passed in a haze of work, the ENT residents were back in the conference room with Dr. Pratt and Dr. Bates. This time, we were assigned seating, grouped by "residency year."

Steve met with them solo. God only knows what they discussed. Tony, Will, and I were grouped together. Nothing like a harsh reminder from the attendings that I wasn't graduating on time and a tell to everyone sitting at the table that I was likely *the snitch*.

"Maybe this investigation will be the best way to enact change, after all," Tony said as he looked at me.

The ice between us had thawed at the resident retreat. Even if we never talked about whatever it was that he wanted to tell me.

"Yeah," Will added. "That'd be nice."

I wondered which of them might've written the anonymous message, searching their faces and body language for some kind of sign.

"I really think it's inappropriate that we do a lot of nursing tasks. Especially after rotating at The Promised Land," I chimed in, feeling emboldened and remembering my six weeks there, which now felt like a dream. "This isn't how it works at other hospitals, and it impacts our education and training."

"Okay, guys," Dr. Pratt said with a heavy sigh. "I understand you are frustrated, but this is the military hospital system. We want to have a residency program here, and we want to make it better, but trust me...the NCRA survey is not the place to make these complaints. We want to maintain our accreditation."

"Yeah, but isn't that why they have the surveys?" Tony pressed.

Tony had to be the other person who reported the program. He *had* to. This would all be so much easier if he could pull me aside and be honest. We could be a team at long last. Part of me felt so vindicated, and another part, frustrated. The entire program was on the line, and they were doing surveys and having meetings instead of digging any deeper.

"You want to graduate from an accredited program," Dr. Bates added. "If you don't, it actually has significant consequences for your career down the road. It's the same thing as being board certified and maintaining your certifications."

The residents and I all glanced at one another, and some of us literally put our heads down, as if this conversation wasn't happening. Yes, we did want to graduate. Yes, we did want to be ENTs. Yes, we did want to help people. But was this the right way to do it? Was this the *only* way? Most of us, unfortunately, were too deep into it to consider any other path. Finish the program. Graduate. Don't ask questions.

"Just because something has been a certain way for so long doesn't make it right," Steve said.

I nodded in appreciation.

"Can't we go to someone higher up in the hospital and say, look, our program's accreditation is being threatened?" Tony asked.

"Yes, actually, we have," Dr. Pratt snapped. "And that's exactly why we are about to hire six brand new techs. And we can order whatever supplies we want. In fact, Sergeant Williams is going to send an email out with a new protocol. You can list all the supplies you think you'll need, and he will order them."

"Sick! All we had to do was complain, and now we get to hire people and order supplies." Tony grinned and leaned back in his chair. Maybe Tony wasn't actually in this fight for the right reasons. He just wanted to punt off his work and make his own life easier.

"Well, yes and no. We have been fighting for this for years," Dr. Bates said.

There were two beats of awkward silence.

Dr. Pratt plastered a fake, conciliatory smile on her face. "Let's all thank Dr. Bates for the four years of hard work and dedication that he has put into this program. I think everyone can acknowledge how much he cares about all of the residents and Main Hospital. He gave his all to make this a better place."

Scattered clapping filled the room.

"Are you happy to be leaving?" I asked when the noise died down. I guess I had nothing left to lose by being so bold. It seemed that everyone knew what I was really asking and wanted someone else to ask it: *Was his departure a choice?*

"Yeah." He paused. "Yeah, I think so."

* * *

January 2022, Main Hospital, Hawaii

The FOIA request finally arrived. I was so busy with all the other drama, I almost forgot about it. Unbelievable. It was the entire investigation that Dr. James conducted about the ENT department at Main Hospital. The 170-page packet detailed interviews with every resident and attending, their identities redacted but their roles obvious.

> To put it bluntly, CPT Neighbors has put this program through hell. Her presence significantly and negatively affects those around her, especially her co-residents. She treats her peers poorly and is not a team player.

Friends

It made my stomach churn. Some of it was blatant fiction. All of it was written to save their own asses. They couldn't possibly know I'd ever read this. Even though I'd suspected this level of nastiness and gaslighting, I still curled up in my bed and cried.

"Handicapped."

* * *

February 2022, Waikiki, Hawaii

Brad and I lounged by the Pineapple Palace Resort's pool. Palm trees swayed gently in the breeze, casting dappled shadows on the turquoise water. It was a world away from the sterile hospital halls and the looming investigation. For a stolen weekend, at least, life felt uncomplicated.

"Mimosa or piña colada?" Brad asked, emerging from the swim-up bar with a grin.

"Both," I replied, unable to choose between the sweet and the bubbly. It was a small decision, but it felt symbolic of my current state of mind—wanting it all, but knowing I couldn't have it. I relished the sweet taste of alcohol and the warmth of the sun on my skin, sinking into what I hoped would be amnesia and maybe even worse—so I wouldn't have to return to all my haters at Main Hospital.

As we sipped our drinks, our conversation drifted to deeper waters. He asked about my family—my least favorite subject. We exchanged some banter about our siblings and my brother's occupation as a video gamer, living at home with my mom. To my surprise, he didn't judge. Said his brother is a musician. Then, Brad opened up about his father's death, his voice thick with emotion. "I was in the OR when I got the news," he said, a tremor in his voice. "They think it was cardiac arrest, but I'll never know for sure."

I reached out and squeezed his hand, a silent offering of comfort. We shared a bond over this loss, a connection that went beyond mere attraction.

"Do you think our dads are in heaven playing chess together?" Brad asked suddenly, a mischievous glint in his eyes.

I laughed, surprised by his question. "Maybe," I said. "Hopefully they're friends."

The laughter bubbled up from within me, a release of tension I hadn't realized I was carrying.

We both laughed a little too loudly, like maniacs. And then I realized that it was the first time in five years—since my dad died—that I had laughed at all about him being dead. My eyes filled up with tears, but I stopped them just in time.

Not when I was actually having some unexpected fun. This wasn't the time or the place to dwell. It was a different kind of pain—like I was healing and hurting all at once.

Friends

As the laughter faded, the familiar empty pang came roaring back. I missed my father, his silly jokes and booming personality. The weekend passed in a blur of sunshine, laughter, and stolen kisses. But as we boarded the plane back to Honolulu, the weight of reality settled back upon me. The investigation, the probation, the crumbling marriage—it was all waiting for me back home.

After the romantic getaway, I was back at it. Mind gaming it with myself. Pacing my condo with the weight of the investigation eating away at me. It was hard to reconcile the carefree joy of the weekend with the looming threat of the NBO inquiry. I reached for my phone, needing the reassurance of a familiar voice.

"Hey, sorry to bother," I said when Paul answered. "Just wanted to update you about the investigation stuff."

We talked for hours, dissecting every detail of the investigation, the things people wrote about me, speculating about who could have sent the anonymous email. Paul, ever the pragmatist, offered his insights and support.

"Maybe it was one of the neurosurgeons," he suggested. "Or Major Ernst. Or even Tony."

"Or Dr. Owens," I added, my voice laced with bitterness. "Maybe even Dr. Bates himself."

"You're never going to figure it out, Cindy. I mean—look—whoever sent you that, clearly doesn't feel comfortable telling you who they are."

TOO MUCH

"No shit. But it's killing me and I need to know."

His words were a comfort, a reminder that I wasn't alone in this fight. But as I hung up the phone, the paranoia and anxiety returned, suffocating me. I paced the room, my mind racing. I needed something to numb the pain. As much as I didn't want to—I reached for some leftover Valease I had prescribed to me shortly after my father passed away. A random doctor on a medicine rotation felt bad and wrote me a prescription. I only had a few pills—so I was going to have to figure out how not to get hooked on sedatives—or sweet talk Dr. Owens into prescribing them to me.

CHAPTER 16

Words

February 2022, Main Hospital

Dr. Bates escorted me to the mahogany table conference room where Dr. Pratt was seated with a stack of papers. This table, these meetings, they'd become all too familiar.

Dread-inducing.

"Cindy, the CCC voted," Dr. Pratt said, her voice measured.

The slap after a blissful weekend away.

The CCC. Was a joke. The CCC was more like Dr. Bates and Dr. Pratt texting each other whatever they felt the night before meeting with me. Where was this CCC? It was never clear to me who this regulatory body was, even though it apparently held my fate in its hands.

I had to remind myself that this was a slippery slope. By questioning some things, I could easily start questioning everything, and then I would lose what little grip I had on the things that mattered, like my passion for justice…and Brad.

And the stack of papers on the table.

TOO MUCH

Termination papers. Of course. What else could they be?

This was it, the moment I had suspected all this time. Or secretly wanted. *Or both* ... Termination was here. I was prepared to feel sadness and anger, but also relief.

For a small moment, I allowed my mind to wander to a future where I didn't live in fear of Dr. Bates or Dr. Pratt. Where I could lounge poolside with Brad. Where I was happy and fulfilled and able to express myself. If the worst thing in the world—termination from the program—happened, I wouldn't be a resident anymore, sure, but I would also maybe be...

"We've decided to place you on a second probation because of your knowledge deficits," Dr. Pratt said.

"What?" I recoiled from my beachside fantasy.

"As you know, there have been some concerns about professionalism, and some other issues that we are still gathering specific feedback about, which we will pass along to you as soon as we have something to share."

I almost laughed in his face at that point. It was all so *meaningless*. I was honestly hoping I could just be terminated. So that I could forget this place and start a new life.

Anywhere else.

A second probation? How many hoops did these people want me to jump through?

"Okay," I said instead. "Where do I sign?"

"Cindy, you should read it."

"No, it's okay. I'll sign it." I wasn't going to fight. I was tired. I felt so numb that I could easily be mistaken for lazy, even. There was no marriage to fight for. Brad was leaving. I had no idea what to do next, so I decided to go with whatever the universe threw into my lap. And that was another probation, apparently.

A new level of nihilism.

But liberating ...?

"Just take a day and read it," Dr. Pratt insisted.

It was like they wanted me to contest it, like they were disappointed I wasn't my usual adversarial self.

It took more energy from me to resist than to agree at that point. Could they not see that? It was more draining for me to take my finger, flip the pages, skim the words, process, and reflect about what this all meant.

This entire program—my fight for a place in it—was becoming more and more traumatic. The constant negativity was a new level of bullying.

To appease, then play nice.

TOO MUCH

I opened the proposal to a random page that contained feedback from the surveys:

> Cindy is erratic and unsafe. She should not back up junior residents. She should not graduate from this program. She is unprofessional and talks down to staff.
>
> The resident room is much happier when Cindy is not here. We think Cindy records our conversations in the resident room.
>
> Cindy has made allegations against this program that aren't true. I will happily testify against Cindy in court.
>
> I would never want her to operate on my loved ones, or even myself. Cindy is dangerous.
>
> Cindy is rude. She yells and drinks too much. While we have never smelled alcohol on her at work, she comes into work acting drunk and there is talk that she has a drinking problem.
>
> Cindy is incredibly moody and unstable.

Nobody ever said these words to my face. But they had no problem writing them anonymously.

I flipped to the last page of the proposal. And I signed.

* * *

March 2022, Main Hospital, Hawaii

We've been taught that traumatic memories are often anchored in childhood and create shock waves that crisscross our adult lives. A couple of weeks passed, and there were still no updates about the NBO investigation.

The Wellspring seemed to be working. When I asked Dr. Owens for Valease, we had to compromise. She prescribed me Kloopeen instead. I was trying my best not to get hooked. It's a longer acting sedative—I told myself it would be okay to take it every other night.

I felt bad, because Dr. Owens trusted me. I don't think she suspected I was so prone to becoming addicted to things so quickly. Sounds naïve but I also figured she'd be too busy to notice that I was asking her to prescribe me a bunch of things.

Dr. Owens had been promoted to the position of the Graduate Director of Medical Education, which meant that she was Dr. Bates's boss. She oversaw all of the residency programs in the hospital and was essentially third in line in Main Hospital's educational leadership hierarchy.

I'd ask her to refill prescriptions after talking to her for the entire hour. Just as my hand was on the doorknob, as she was rushing to her next appointment, so it was hard for her to say no. Like it was a routine thing for her to prescribe, so she wouldn't have time to question it. I know it sounds terrible. I manipulated her.

Aside from that fact, because she had moved on up in the ranks of the hospital, she probably shouldn't have been my psychiatrist any longer. Our relationship was a legal and ethical conflict of interest.

"I will still see you, but I won't be taking on new patients," she reassured me as we unpacked what her promotion meant. It was confusing. Did she have something to gain from seeing me? It felt like I was the one scoring endless supplies of prescriptions and possibly an ally in the debunked system.

"Dr. Bates is stepping down as program director." I informed her one day.

"I had no idea," she admitted.

Things weren't adding up. "I'm going to talk to him about that," she added.

* * *

April 2022, Main Hospital, Hawaii

One Friday night, I was on call, wasting precious time figuring out this new computer system. A quick bathroom break turned into a frantic dash when Dr. Bates called about Mr. Tomai, a post-op patient with a severely obstructed airway.

I rushed to the Surgical ICU, the room packed with medical staff. Mr. T was struggling to breathe. I quickly assessed the situation and realized he needed an emergency tracheostomy.

With the patient's life hanging in the balance, I made the incision, inserted the trach tube, and inflated the cuff. We manually ventilated him, and his vitals slowly stabilized. Dr. Bates rushed in. His face was pale, and he immediately scanned the vitals. He looked from the tube I was holding to a small amount of blood on the patient's neck and then to the monitor.

"Oh, no," he muttered under his breath.

"Dr. Bates," I said.

"Does he have an airway?" he asked the room.

"Yes." I showed him that the tube was secured.

Dr. Bates started eloquently commanding the room, asking about the patient's lines, whether he was stable to transition to the OR, and if we had a team ready to go. We all shifted into surgery mode.

Dr. Pratt arrived. I'll never forget the question she asked, "So, why the trach?"

I almost froze right there in the hallway, except I had to keep ventilating the patient.

So, why the trach? I'd saved his life while both attendings were missing in action! I started word-vomiting the entire scene to justify what I had done, and as I was speaking, I started to worry that I'd made a wrong move.

Of course, I could have attempted a different airway first, as we typically went from least invasive method in the airway algorithm to the most drastic, but the patient was combative, and his vitals were dropping precipitously. Only a few seconds of poor perfusion to the brain could result in long-term damage, especially at this patient's age. Thankfully, there were no hypoxic effects in this case, but there easily could have been.

TOO MUCH

On the way home that night, I felt shitty about my decision to place a trach. Dr. Bates called. I couldn't really take another chewing out at that point. I answered, almost wincing.

"Cindy, I want you to know that I am *so* proud of you."

"What?" I tried to focus on his words while not veering into the guardrail.

"You did the right thing. I just want you to know that over the next few days, weeks, maybe even months, you will replay this scene in your head over and over and over, and you will go through and pick at all the little things you could have done differently, or better, or maybe you'll ask yourself if you did something wrong. I want you to know that this is totally normal, Cindy. I've been there. These are life-changing events, trust me. And these are the cases that you will want to remember because you learn from them. I wanted to make sure and tell you, Cindy, that I am proud of you because, at the end of the day, no matter what happens with the probation and the rest of the program, that patient has an airway, and he is alive…because of you. You did the right thing."

Dr. Bates knew exactly what to say to make me feel better and take the sting out of Dr. Pratt's disapproval. He knew exactly what my doubts were and what my inner critic was already saying.

I didn't let on, but I had tears in my eyes to hear this teaching, this compassion, this mentorship. It was all I'd ever wanted from him. He was validating my own gut instincts. What a gift.

"Thank you, sir."

Words

Even though it was nice to be praised and validated, deep down, I couldn't help but feel haunted by Dr. Pratt questioning me in the OR. *Why. The. Trach.* I kept asking myself the same thing. Replaying the scene. The airway algorithm. The patient *had* bilateral vocal cord paralysis, *didn't he?*

And then the paranoia.

What if I effed up in the heat of the moment? What if I'd made a mistake? I spiraled. I couldn't help but question, even more, every little detail of that evening. Every choice I had made. Did he or didn't he have true bilateral vocal cord paralysis? Could I trust what I saw with my scope exam? What if the program was right about me and I didn't have the skills to be an ENT? *What if it was it all in my head?*

The next week, I was berated by a few attendings about my clinical decision-making. Someone told me that the patient could have died because of my actions. So even though the patient was alive, I was still wrong. Because he could have died?

No matter what Dr. Bates told me that night, every other comment from the other attendings, the questioning from Dr. Pratt—that's what stuck. All of it echoed the accusations from my mother about how I killed my father. About how Paul lost his case. About how everything is my fault. Maybe they were right. Maybe I was handicapped.

* * *

May 2022, Napali Coast, Hawaii

The raft boat skimmed across the turquoise water, the wind whipping through my hair as we cruised along the majestic Napali Coast. Brad booked this excursion as a surprise, a much-needed escape. The sun kissing my skin, the salt on my lips, and Brad's fingers grazing mine—almost made me forget my next nightmare investigation.

The boat slowed to admire a pod of spinner dolphins, their sleek bodies playfully dancing and arching. Tourists squealed and snapped away, but Brad and I sat back, sharing a soft kiss. It was so touristy of us to do something like this, but, back home, we rarely saw the light of day—or each other.

The mountains were breathtaking, luscious and green, untouched, spiritual bliss. The boat coasted for miles until we stopped to explore the vibrant coral teeming with tropical life.

"We should get a boat and sail around the world and never come back," Brad mused, his eyes sparkling with adventure.

The thought resonated with me, a dream I'd once shared with Paul. But now it felt different. Less like a distant fantasy, more like a tangible possibility. Staring at the mountain range behind him, the waves lapping, cool water so perfectly swirling on my skin—that would be nice. To leave and never go back to anything else, again.

"Yeah," I sighed, a wistful longing in my voice. "Maybe someday."

We snorkeled some more with turtles, eels, and fish, then waded to the shore, shared apple slices and bottled water, the simple pleasure amplified by the vast ocean looking back at us.

Brad chuckled and squeezed my hand. "It's been a rough year. Sorry

I don't have more free time," he said, his gaze drifting towards the horizon. "Did you hear? Ryan is in some serious shit for his DUI."

"DUI?" I asked, my heart sinking.

Brad nodded, his expression grim. "Yeah, he's in a program now and can't take call. It's been tough on us, covering for him."

He recounted the details of Ryan's drunken escapades, the missed shifts, and the blackout nights. A familiar pang of guilt and worry washed over me, reminding me of Kyle's struggles.

"I'm sure he knows you guys care," I offered, hoping to ease Brad's guilt. "By helping him, you're showing him that you're there for him."

"Yeah, I hope so," he said softly.

The conversation shifted to their program director and her relaxed attitude towards the residents' occasional partying.

"We all party," Brad said with a shrug. "Don't you?"

"Sometimes," I admitted, "but it's not always... easy."

Brad's gaze softened. "I get it," he said. "Sometimes, you just need to turn off your brain for a while."

His words struck a chord within me.

"Do you ever think people do drugs to turn off their brains

sometimes?" I asked. "Like they use because everything is too much for them, and they need a break from it all?"

Brad nodded slowly. "Totally. I had a roommate in college like that. Brilliant guy, but he couldn't handle life. He felt he had to do drugs, too. I found him dead one morning. An overdose."

A heavy silence fell between us. We sat there, side by side, two souls connected by a shared understanding of pain and loss. The sun dipped lower in the sky, casting long shadows across the water. The beauty of the moment felt fragile, fleeting.

As we boarded the plane back to Honolulu that evening, I couldn't shake the feeling that this idyllic escape was just a temporary reprieve. The reality of my life—the investigation, the probation, the crumbling marriage—awaited me back on Oahu.

But for now, I clung to the memory of the dolphins, the laughter, and the shared moments of connection with Brad. It was a reminder that even in the darkest of times, there could still be moments of joy and connection.

* * *

May 2022, Main Hospital, Hawaii

"Cindy, did you get paged on the call pager that night about Mr. T?" Dr. Bates asked at our next probation meeting.

"Yes, why?"

"Because we got a complaint about it. They said that they paged about his stridor and it took five minutes to get a response."

"I went up there right away. You called me, and I ran up there with a scope. Usually, we aren't even in the hospital, because we take home call. It just so happened I was in the clinic making templates."

"Ultimately, you did. We are just trying to find out if there's a problem with the pager so we can fix it, that's all. You're not in trouble." Dr. Bates leaned forward and smiled.

"The page did come through while I was walking there, if that's helpful," I added.

"Cindy, there's one more thing." Dr. Pratt looked over at Dr. Bates and said, "Let me address this."

"You know we got cited by NCRA, right?" Dr. Pratt asked.

"Yes."

"One of the citations was for allowing our program to be impacted by other learners, to the detriment of all involved," Dr. Pratt said. "In our investigation, we found out that the other learner was you." She gave me a look.

"We did a Google survey and got some answers from your co-residents," Dr. Bates added. "They said you are unpredictable."

The anonymous comments had bothered me for months. It all felt like one giant game to eject me from the program. But then it snapped into focus with stunning clarity.

What Gracie said. *I was "predictably unpredictable."*

I thought about everything that had happened. My marriage. Paul's case. My friendships. My relationship with my family. My work.

The common denominator was me. What if everyone was right?

What if I had single-handedly destroyed the program? All of the events of the last few years seemed to fit that narrative. What if there wasn't another, more malicious narrative? What if *their* narrative was the right one, after all?

I chose to welcome certain people and situations into my life because that's who and what I thought I deserved. I chose to keep trying to fix problem after problem in my residency program, even though I knew, deep down, that the systemic issues would never change. Still, my role was to be a resident. I had overstepped my role. I hadn't stayed in my lane. And in doing that, in upsetting people and defying authority, I inadvertently gave power to the men in my workplace when I should have just focused on my job.

My self-empowerment could've taken the form of gaining knowledge, rather than caring so much about my appearance and sexuality. I also chose to use my mental illness as a crutch and an excuse, but only when it was convenient for me.

I chose to be lazy when I was too tired to push myself and work harder. I chose to drink alcohol because it was easier to numb the pain than it was to sit there, dig deep, and admit that I had made mistakes.

Because then I would have had to figure out how to fix myself. But that was the true work ahead of me, no matter what happened with the program. Pushing it off didn't actually change that I needed to grow as a doctor and a person.

I chose to betray the people I cared about and use people's secrets against them so that I could feel better about myself, only to have it backfire against me. Then I acted surprised, like a victim, rather than the hero of my own story.

* * *

June 2022, Main Hospital, Hawaii

The program announced another round of NCRA surveys, and I was required to participate. I answered honestly but the notion that anything could actually change was dead in the water. My humiliation complete, I wanted to put it all behind me.

A week later, Charli announced to the group that, "We went from like 50% satisfaction to perfect scores. Well, *almost* perfect scores." And then she cut her eyes over to me.

The residents had apparently all agreed to answer 5/5 on every question so that the program could maintain its accreditation and so that they could graduate without completely invalidating their residencies. Or, at least, so everyone else could graduate.

TOO MUCH

Nobody had told me about this plan, as things between me and my peers weren't exactly gelling at that point, and so I looked like the asshole.

"You can see the results?" Dr. Bates sat up from his slumped position in the corner. He almost seemed nervous about it.

"Yeah." She smiled. "I accidentally came across the response spreadsheet when I was logging my cases!"

When I went back to my computer, I realized why Dr. Bates was so nervous. The percentages on the survey that allegedly led to the NCRA issuing its citations were as follows:

> Education compromised by non-physician related obligations: 50%
> Inter-professional teamwork skills modeled or taught: 60%
> Taught about healthcare disparities: 50%
> Instruction to recognize fatigue and burnout: 70%
> And finally:
> Impact from other learners: 80%

I recalled what I had been told during the interview by the NBO executives. It seemed cryptic at the time, but now it all made sense: *"Cindy, we work very closely with the NCRA. You're familiar with the National Council for Residency Accreditation..."*

I didn't make anything of it at the time, but things were starting to add up. Maybe it wasn't just my emails. Or just the surveys.

The power of my whistleblowing had intersected with the unfolding of things that were never in my control. All that with Tony's comment about *radical change*. Maybe the radical change didn't just need to happen inside of me.

I didn't know what to think anymore, which left a void where my conflicting ideas and inner demons could take over.

The voices in my head were getting louder. I was listening.

CHAPTER 17

Answers

July 2022, Oahu Yacht Club, Hawaii

The day I'd been trying to manifest for myself for years was finally here, but it looked like nothing I had envisioned.

I wasn't graduating.

It was supposed to be my day, in some grand ballroom someplace extra like the Four Seasons, decked out in a haku lei getting congratulated by everyone. People would be saying they were so happy I made it after all these years. Instead, we were here. At the Oahu Yacht Club—celebrating Steve's solo graduation.

I stood in the breezeway, watching him recite his speech from his perfectly organized journal. Reminded me of when we were second year residents. I actually bought the same journal as his—these fancy black ones—he said he wrote every thought down that would come into his mind, so it wouldn't bother him anymore, that's the only way it could escape him…it helped me to do the same sometimes.

Steve's daughter tugged at my dress. Her big blue eyes filled with pure innocence. She had no idea all of this was a farce. The wife clung onto their newborn, swaying in the breezeway. Maybe his oldest knew I needed love and energy in that cold moment.

Answers

"Carry me! Carry me!" she squealed.

Reluctantly, I picked her up and swayed his little girl in my arms. The gentle waves in the background and her giggles helped drown out the bullshit of Steve thanking his wife and the bullshit of Dr. Pratt praising Steve for being a hard worker all these years. The same years I had been there, apparently hardly working.

The girl's loving vibes were a shield and a comfort.

A gulf opened between me and the world. I had none of the things Steve had. And yet we started out together. I thought I could have it all. Instead I had no spouse. No children. No graduation. No praise. No respect.

I had gotten so close. I tried to convince myself that I was genuinely happy. Perhaps it was better this way. I was no longer married to someone I resented. I wasn't at the podium, saying bullshit and thanking people who had actually made my life shittier, all while showing off my biggest, fakest smile.

Was my alienation a relief? A punishment? All of the above?

Later than night, I received an unexpected text from an old friend, Evan:

Hey, want to get high?

Bitterness rose up within me again. Sure, I knew that self-medicating was the wrong choice, but I had just watched my co-resident graduate without me. My own future was up in the air. I wanted to go to the very edge and see if I could make it back.

Did I care?

I almost thought about texting Paul. Instead, I sent Evan a text inviting him over to my condo. Then I aimlessly walked around my living room while I waited for him, almost on autopilot, trying not to worry about the oblivion that was about to swallow me up.

It's wild how someone can pop back into your life after years and it's like they haven't aged a day, mentally or physically. Evan leaned back against the plush cushions of my couch, a contented sigh escaping his lips. The city lights twinkled below, a mesmerizing tapestry of urban life that felt a million miles away from the sterile confines of the hospital.

"Remember that night at the beach house?" Evan asked, a mischievous glint in his eyes. "We were so close..."

I chuckled, the memory flooding back. Years ago, we almost hooked up. Our friendship teetering on the edge of something more. But the timing had never been right. And now, he was married, his life a world away from mine.

"Yeah," I said, a bittersweet smile touching my lips. "But some things are just not meant to be."

Evan reached for my hand, his fingers intertwining with mine. "Maybe not," he whispered, his voice husky with desire. "But that doesn't mean we can't still have a little fun."

He pulled out a small vial, the white powder gleaming under the dim light. My heart skipped a beat. Cocaine. My old friend.

"I can't," I said.

Evan's eyes softened. "I know," he said, his voice filled with understanding. "Sorry—I can leave."

The temptation was overwhelming. I longed to escape the pain, the loneliness, the crushing weight of my failures. I wanted to feel that rush of euphoria, that fleeting moment of oblivion.

"No, I mean—you came all this way—I want to." I said, my voice barely audible.

A beat of silence and the weight of our shared past. The only sound was the distant hum of the city below.

With a shared glance, a silent agreement passed between us. Evan opened the vial, his hands steady as he carefully crafted two lines onto the glass coffee table. Then he rolled a crisp bill, the anticipation building with each passing second. He offered me the first line.

I took a deep breath, steeling myself for the familiar rush. The sharp sting burned and then left a bitter aftertaste. And then—blissfully numb. Until the next one. We indulged, the white powder blurring the lines between reality and fantasy. Talking for hours, our conversation a jumbled mix of shared memories, regrets, and unspoken desires. It was the typical cocaine afterhours podcast talking up dreams, ambitions, the paths we had chosen and the ones we had left behind.

TOO MUCH

As the first rays of dawn arrived, we stumbled onto the balcony, the cool morning air a welcome relief from the stifling heat of the apartment. We stood in silence, our gazes fixed on the city below.

"I envy you," Evan said.

I turned to him, surprised. "Why?"

"You're a doctor," he said, his voice filled with a longing that mirrored my own. "You make a difference in people's lives. You have a purpose."

I laughed, a bitter, hollow sound. "You have a beautiful wife, a successful career, a life most people would dream of," I said. "How could you possibly envy me?"

Evan sighed, his shoulders slumping. "It's not what it seems," he said, his voice heavy with regret. "I'm getting divorced, Cindy. My life—it's a mess."

Every day, people go around envying the lives of others when they have no idea what is really going on under the surface. These constant "what ifs" and comparisons f*** up our parameters of happiness and success. The lies. The truth. None of this is glamorous. This is nothing like *Grey's Anatomy*.

We stood in silence, two lost souls gazing out at the vast expanse of the city, yearning for something more, something real.

* * *

Answers

July 2022, Hawaii

When nightlife started up again post-Covid, there wasn't a lot going on. To celebrate another year of residency ending, a bunch of us splurged on a table. I dug out a cute, skanky dress, a relic from pre-Covid days. We hit the town hard, like we were in college without a care in the world. Made friends with some tourists.

Five minutes after walking into the club, a friend of a friend offered our group Xax, Molly, Coke...Addy. Didn't feel like revisiting the cocaine scene, so I opted for what I rationalized as the next best legal thing: Addfocus.

"This is a safe space," the girl drunkenly reassured me in the bathroom stall. Her boobs were busting out of her mini dress—her skin soft, slathered in coconut oil. She smelled like Chanel. The music thumped outside the stall, the bass vibrating through the thin walls. She crushed a pill and we snorted the white chalk from a key. As dingy and dirty as it all was, it felt safe with her. Her presence was magnetic, and I found myself imagining a future where we were inseparable.

"Where are you from?" I whispered. Not trying to be rude, but I could tell she wasn't from Hawaii.

"New York."

The bathroom stall felt safer than my home with Paul—and safer than my residency ever did. Not that I was scared anything bad would happen to me, but even if something did happen, I didn't care. I'd rather die having fun. After numbing out with Evan the other day,

TOO MUCH

I found myself craving some more pain relief. Rushing me with illicit guilty pleasure.

"Wow, I've always wanted to go—I mean—like live there—thank you." She slipped her pills back into her purse and we washed our hands, made our way back to the table. Before I could get her number, she disappeared into the big group of dancing strangers thumping to the music and flashing lights.

"I ordered vodka sodas and a bottle of champagne!" Jennifer squealed.

Brad and I caressed each other, laughing like it didn't matter whether or not we were a couple and that he was off to fellowship in a few weeks. Our magical time together was drawing to an end, but I didn't want to think about it. Very high school. My brain was off.

* * *

July 2022, Main Hospital, Hawaii

The fluorescent lights in Dr. Owens's office stabbed at my eyes, each flicker reminding me I needed more Addfocus. The sterile scent of disinfectant replaced the usual comforting aroma of dark chocolate, and even the bookshelves cluttered with plants seemed to judge my deceit.

"Cindy," Dr. Owens began, her voice cool and detached, "I want to know how you're doing but before I forget, I have some news regarding the cheating allegations."

I clenched my jaw, wishing I could disappear. All I wanted was another prescription, a quick fix for the gnawing anxiety and the impending crash.

Dr. Owens leaned forward, a sly smile playing on her lips. "Word on the street is, only a handful of those copied answers were actually correct."

Disbelief washed over me. Had we all been duped? I watched as Dr. Owens unwrapped a piece of dark chocolate, her movements slow and deliberate, like a taunt.

"So, what happens now?" I asked.

"Who knows?" she shrugged, popping the chocolate into her mouth. "Things are always changing in this hospital."

Her nonchalant attitude sent a shiver down my spine. Was she implying that the consequences might not be as severe as we feared? Or was she just messing with me?

"Anyway," I managed, pushing down the rising panic, "I've been having trouble focusing lately. I was thinking of getting evaluated for ADD."

Dr. Owens's eyes narrowed, her gaze piercing through my façade. "Tell me about your history with Addfocus," she said, her voice laced with suspicion.

I wove a tale of academic struggles and sleepless nights, each word coated in desperation. Dr. Owens scanned me carefully, her expression unreadable. Finally, with a sigh, she got up to order the prescription into the computer system.

Fifteen minutes later, I was in the hospital bathroom, the bitter taste of Addfocus burning my nostrils. The familiar rush of energy masked the shame and guilt, but only for a moment. Deep down, I knew this was just another temporary fix, another step down a dangerous path. But I was desperate for to make it through the day.

* * *

July 2022, Hawaii

I ran my hands over Brad's bare chest as a brilliant sunrise crested over the horizon. Even though I hoped this wouldn't be the last time our naked bodies were tangled together, something told me that I wouldn't be seeing him again. He was leaving for fellowship that night.

"Good morning," I whispered.

He kissed me on the forehead chastely. "Hi. I woke up with a sore throat, sorry. I don't want to get you sick."

"Mine is too, actually," I said, surprised to realize it after taking a quick bodily inventory.

"We probably drank too much," he said with a naughty laugh. "Do you want some water?"

"Sure." I fell quiet for a moment. "Can I give you a ride to the airport later?"

"You'll still be at work, right?"

"Yeah. I'm not feeling super great, though. I can always call out."

"Sure, I mean, if you want."

I didn't like his noncommittal tone, so I decided to make a risky pivot. "Hey, how about I visit you in Boston?"

"Cindy, we talked about this. I don't want to make any plans right now. Can you just let me get settled in, get my apartment, do boards, and then we can talk about it?"

I knew his ask was reasonable, but I worried there was a deeper reason behind it. That he didn't want me to visit at all, that this had just been a fling. This was where my relationships always went bad—when I started to be vulnerable. I regretted getting involved with him in the first place. Now he would be just another person who left me. Another person I fell for only to lose them. Another person for me to chase, beg, and cry over, while they moved on and forgot about me.

"Yeah, no problem." I cleared my throat.

He threw his shirt and pants on, and I tried not to wonder why he wasn't trying to have sex with me one last time. I realized that I was trying desperately to reinforce the connection between us. Nothing good ever came from desperation. I decided to back off. Instead, I wrapped myself in sweats, walked him to the elevator, and that was that.

When I got back to my empty condo, I crushed up the little white pill, snorted a line, and hopped in the shower. Then it dawned on me: the reason why I couldn't seem to stay high. I was always chasing the next best feeling.

This was the vicious cycle of addiction that I found myself in all over again. I wanted to achieve greatness: the perfect husband, the high-rise condo, the cars, the clothes, the handbags, invitations to the best parties, the best job…so I could feel like someone.

But most of all, I wanted to make my parents proud. I wanted to prove myself. And in doing that, I was edging closer to death. Not just an emotional death or a spiritual death. I felt my own physical death approaching.

The truth hit me fresh every morning when I woke up: no matter what I achieved, what I obtained, I never felt good enough. I never felt seen. I was never happy or proud of myself.

Getting high became a way to escape my depression and self-loathing. It helped me forget the fact that I felt trapped. I couldn't kill myself because it would make everyone upset. I couldn't quit because that would also make everyone upset—or relieved, and I didn't want them to have that. I had to keep going, but I needed to make it bearable. This was the only way I knew how to do it.

This was how I would throw jet fuel into the tank until I self-combusted. I felt like an airplane stuck in limbo on the tarmac, engine idling, but never allowed to take off, never allowed to park. Eventually, something would have to give.

I was swirling in a vortex of pain and confusion. I was the danger.

Erratic. Unpredictable. Maybe I did need help. Maybe I was too crazy to be a doctor. Too stupid to ignore the truth. Too smart to ignore it. Too psychotic to stop thinking. Too beautiful to fade away.

All around, in every way, I was cursed with being *too much.*

And what had I done with it? I tried to destroy it. I tried to smother it. I tried to drug it up. I tried to work it to death. I tried to act as if it didn't exist. I tried to hate it. Then I tried to get everyone else to hate it. I tried to love it. I tried to embrace it. Nothing worked.

Was I functional? I could be, especially if I could control myself. But that was the crux of the issue. I was never enough.

I didn't know if I could hold on any longer or whether that control could last. I had to commit to controlling myself every single day, and some days, I just didn't have it in me.

I called in sick after my shower, and the next day, I woke up with my phone in my hands, still streaming some random show from the night before, when I'd passed out in exhaustion. I was feeling truly ill, the tornado in my brain finally overshadowed by fevers wracking my body. I was honestly surprised I had made it through the night. Part of me was disgusted: *Fuck, I'm still here.* The other part was relieved: *Fuck, I'm still here!*

I had to go to work that day, but my body felt off. Something was different. No matter how much Addfocus I took, I couldn't get back to baseline.

* * *

TOO MUCH

July 2022, Main Hospital, Hawaii

The next day, I walked into the resident room feeling like trash.

"Morning," I mumbled to the room as I snuck past my co-residents to my desk in the corner.

"Morning," Maria sung.

The other residents ignored me. It must have been nice to pretend that I wasn't actually a senior resident.

"Hey." Tony appeared at my desk as I was logging into my computer.

"What's up?"

"They ran the tests on Mr. T over the weekend."

"Really? Why?"

"To confirm whether he has true vocal cord paralysis—you know—they want to consider—"

"Shut up. And?"

"He has bilateral vocal cord paralysis," Tony offered a warm smile. As if it was any consolation prize. Like he knew I was struggling to search for the truth—somewhere between my paranoia and instincts.

This time I was right. I did the right thing. But it didn't feel as good to be vindicated if the program still made me question myself so deeply.

Answers

And being right wasn't a victory. It was the beginning of a long recovery for the patient.

CHAPTER 18

Millions

August 2022, Kaka'ako, Hawaii

It's been five years of residency. Can you believe it? Time flies. And I've accomplished nothing.

My apartment feels extra empty with Bradley Brown gone. The sheets still soaked in his cologne. Nothing feels alive. It hasn't since Paul left, if I'm being honest. I can't think about the void right now because I feel so shitty—physically. Pretty sure I finally got Covid.

Clicking around on Instacart, I add whatever looks good for sick people: fruits, veggies, OJ, vitamins, soup, premade salads, nuts. For the last five years, I've been surviving off pills, caffeine, water, packaged overly-processed food, and snacks from the nurses. Gifted food from patients, sometimes.

I stopped visiting my Kyle and my mom on a regular basis years ago because I needed to dissociate "normal people" and their lifestyle from "hospital people." People at work seemed to be obsessed with my personal life. Asking if I went to the same high school as a former President, when I was going to have kids, why Paul got out of the military, what ethnicity I was, if my mom had a job, and where. It all felt very stalker-vibes, especially when people asked to see pictures of my friends and family. Paul and I made a pact of no photos, videos, or social media posts—to be invisible online.

My temperature is 101.4. A legitimate fever. Three days in bed roll by. Sweating, waking up, checking the time, and wondering why my phone isn't blowing up. Does anyone care if I'm alive?

Don't feel like eating. Rummage through the odds and ends of leftover meds and puff my inhaler. Roll over on my side.

Brad is in Boston, but I text him that I'm sick.

Go to the ER, he texts back.

* * *

August 2022, Main Hospital Emergency Room, Hawaii

When I arrive, I'm ushered to a room in the back corner and one of the nurses promptly places an IV in my arm. "If it's okay, the doctor ordered you some fluids."

An attending peeks in the doorway. "Hi, Cindy, sorry you're feeling so bad. I'm filling out the EUA paperwork right now, and we'll get you out of here. Is there anything else I can get you? Pain meds?"

"Do you think I need a chest X-Ray?"

"No, no. I really don't. It won't change anything." He pauses. "But if you want one, it's no big deal. Happy to order it. Happy to."

"Oh, gosh, no please. If you don't think it's necessary, then no need. I was only wondering because of the asthma history, is all."

"All of us in the ER that qualified took Palovia, and it knocked out the Covid symptoms within forty-eight hours. You'll feel much better, okay?" He smiles and adds, "Now I'll get this signed off, and by the time those fluids are done, you'll be on your way."

Within thirty minutes of checking in, I'm out the door with medication for Covid recovery. I feel privileged. Millions of people in the United States died from the virus, and here I am, rushed to a private room in the ER because I'm a resident.

Does that make it okay? I don't know. Even so, I feel guilty. Guilty for being privileged. Like someone else out there deserves this medication more than I do, even though, I am legitimately sick.

And so begins my spiral.

As soon as I'm untethered from the toxic environment of Main Hospital and I'm all alone, there's nothing to do but think about why and how I got so sick.

* * *

September 10, 2022, West Oahu

"Dr. Bates? Sorry to bother you on a Saturday," I say, my voice tight as I rummage through my kitchen junk drawer for a pen and paper. Medical books, pens, maps, flashlights, and food wrappers spill across my counters. This isn't how I wanted to spend my weekend, but the weight of what's happening is suffocating.

"Hi Cindy... is everything okay?" he asks, his voice cautious.

I put him on speaker and open the group text thread on my phone, my heart pounding. Will, one of my co-residents, had sent a meme: a bald eagle, wrapped in an American flag, sitting at a table, eating pancakes.

"No. No, it's not okay. This can't wait until Monday," I say, gripping the phone so tightly my knuckles turn white.

"What is it?" he asks, his voice laced with concern.

"The group texts! They're relentless. It's harassment, bullying, and it has to stop." My voice rises as I recount the constant barrage of messages, the thinly veiled insults, and the uncomfortable feeling of being targeted. "You said I was unprofessional. But all of this is unprofessional!"

I scribble down the date and time of the meme, a record of this latest offense. "I know this sounds insane, but this meme is directed at me," I explain, my voice shaking. "It's referencing a conversation I had with Maria about breakfast yesterday. How did Will know to send this image in a group text?"

A long silence hangs in the air. "Cindy," Dr. Bates says slowly, "don't you think it's just an eagle because it's September eleventh?"

"But it's not!" I snap. "It's the tenth! You have to believe me."

I can hear the doubt in his voice, the dismissal. It's a familiar feeling, one that fuels the growing anger in my chest.

"I know you won't believe me," I say, my voice heavy with resignation. "But this meme is not a coincidence. It's part of a pattern, and it's not okay."

"We'll look into it," Dr. Bates assures me.

But I know he won't. It's my word against theirs, and the truth is getting harder and harder to see through the fog of their manipulation.

I take screenshots and send them to Paul. As much as I hate to keep him involved in this, he's the only one who knows the depth of the situation, so I keep him in the loop. The termination, the allegations. The investigations. The comments.

* * *

September 20, 2022, Main Hospital, Hawaii

My intern, Maria, her blonde ponytail bobbing slightly, taps gently on the other side of the wooden exam room door. "Cindy? How are you feeling?"

It is two in the morning, and as the chief resident, I am supervising Maria on night call. We have a post-op patient in clinic for a nosebleed, five days after a routine nose job. I can hear their muffled conversation a few rooms over, and it seems like everything is fine. That is why I have chosen to step away. "Just a minute! I will be right there," I call out, trying to keep my voice even.

Millions

Alone in the darkened exam room, I hold an ultrasound probe to my neck, listening to my breath and the slight pinging of the high-frequency waveforms confirming what I already suspect...yes, my lymph nodes are indeed enlarged.

I have felt some lumps in my neck a few days ago. In my current state of mind, I have decided, *What better time than now to ultrasound myself?*

A cluster of white nodes glows back at me from the screen. They do not look right. Too cloudy, too gray, with ill-defined borders, and the largest one has a floating necrotic center. It is bigger than two centimeters and more round than oval. The debris floats back and forth in sync with my heartbeat. It almost looks like the node is invading surrounding muscles and tissues.

I know it. Cancer. Classic textbook metastases. In my head, it is cancer until proven otherwise.

I am screwed. My life is over.

Never mind this residency program. Or Paul, my ex-husband, moving in with his new girlfriend. Never mind the inevitable termination letter looming. Then a discharge from the Army. At least I will not have to pay back my medical school debt to Uncle Sam when I am finally dead.

When I am dead, I can stop fighting.

This is all because I have not followed up on that breast MRI three years ago. I was thirty-three years old and have decided that "just a lump" does not warrant follow-up. Or maybe it is because of the divorce. Because I was forced to repeat a residency year. Because it is too late.

Sure, nobody has told me what the breast lump is. Nobody has told me I actually have a diagnosis of cancer. But, the lump... I have always suspected it. Something coming. If not the Army, then cancer. What a sick joke.

I move the ultrasound probe to my thyroid gland and notice tiny white specks. Calcifications. Nothing looks normal.

The ultrasound jelly cold on my neck. The tears, hot on my face. I don't make a sound. Even though, I think my life is going to be over soon. How did I miss this?

Maria and the patient's voices grow louder down the hall. I switch on the light, turn off the ultrasound, and wipe down the machine and my neck. Then, I wipe my eyes and face, pasting on a forced smile as I head to the exam room.

Maria and I peer inside the patient's nose with a flexible scope. No bleeding. The patient is in tears.

"It is going to be okay," Maria reassures her. I can feel Maria looking at me, wondering if I'm okay. She's clever and intuitive like that. I try not to sniffle. The patient sniffles and it relieves me—assuming Maria won't notice I'm a little high, or coming down. Can't even tell which is which anymore since I'm feeling a little paranoid. Try to compose myself.

"You are going to be just fine," I add, echoing her sentiment despite the turmoil raging inside me.

I feel like a massive hypocrite reassuring her because nothing feels okay at all. Everyone thinks I am losing it, and now, maybe...I am. Instead of running down the hall and screaming at the top of my lungs, I force another smile and play the role of chief resident. I grab an ice pack because ice packs always make nose job patients feel better, even if they do not need them.

I look at Maria and remind her that this whole situation has been an epic waste of my rapidly dwindling time. "There is no major source of bleeding, so just have her wait a few more minutes, take another look, and she should be good to go. The splints probably just irritated the mucosa. It is very common to have some bleeding after a surgery like this."

I walk out the door, forgetting to say goodbye to the patient.

I wish an ice pack could help me. At least I am going to Boston next week, where they have good doctors.

* * *

September 22, 2022, Main Hospital, Hawaii

"I'm not a terrorist," I mutter to Dr. Owens.

She's one of them.

They say I'm paranoid. Delusional. Mentally ill.

TOO MUCH

What if I'm the only one seeing things clearly?

Pothos plants crawl up Dr. Owens's bookshelves. The jar of candy sitting on the table between us is killing me. I'm so hopped up on this combo of Addfocus and Kloopeen, I have to pace around. Can't tell if I am thinking clearly, but...*I think I am.*

Dr. Owens laughs, then peers over her glasses with her soft brown eyes. "What?"

She's been my psychiatrist for at least three years now. It's disappointing that she isn't taking me seriously. Of all people. She should know better. "They're spreading rumors...saying I'm something...something I am not."

I stop pacing to look out her office windows at the green mountains that face Pearl Harbor.

She stares at me intently. "Go on..."

"It's because I said something on the phone to Dr. Bates. He mentioned September eleventh. I would never hurt *anyone*. If anyone around here is having delusions, it's them—shared delusional disorder!" I pull my bun out and toss my hospital ID badge into my Louis Vuitton purse.

"Cindy, I don't think—"

"I'm not stupid—or crazy. I have cancer, but they won't tell me. You people want me to find out at another hospital. Like when I go to

Boston for that conference next week. None of you can look me in the eye."

She leans forward in her chair. She's wearing the newest Army uniform with her legs crossed, a full bird colonel, staring me down. "Cindy, you know you don't have to go to Boston."

I scoff and sit back down. She's a doctor, yet when I say I'm dying, she doesn't seem to care. "Why? So I can *die*? That'd solve several problems for you all, wouldn't it?"

"Cindy, I can assure you—"

"Do you think I need to be admitted to the psych ward?" I interrupt.

"I can offer you admission, but do you really want to run away to the psych ward?" Psychiatric textbooks crowd the shelves behind her.

"No, but…"

"Do you need any refills on your meds?" She smiles.

"Yes, actually…I do. Kloopeen…" I say, staring at the lush backdrop. "And Addfocus."

Something about this visit feels fake. Too easy. Like it's all part of a massive set-up. The termination proposal is looming any day now. I can feel it. I just…know. I get up again, but this time, I'm leaving. "You know what would be nice? If someone around here told me the fucking goddamn truth!" Tears spring to my eyes despite me fighting them.

TOO MUCH

"Cindy!"

"What?"

"Cindy, you are having an acute stress reaction right now. It seems you are having *delusions*—"

"You know who is having delusions? *Them!*" I stab my finger in the direction of the Main Hospital command offices.

"We can get you on some additional medication, temporarily. Give you some time off. Do you feel well enough to go to Boston? You can make up the trauma course later."

Dr. Owens rises but I charge toward the door, wiping hot tears from my face.

"Honestly, are you even listening? I said I have cancer. Nobody cares about anything I ever say. Nobody wants to take call. I'm the *bad guy*. I'm the one on *drugs*. I'm suddenly the *alcoholic*. How convenient! Now you people want me to resign? Guess what! I'm *never* going to resign!" I throw open the door, freedom just a step away. Maybe. Part of me wonders whether I'll ever be truly free. The target had grown so big on my back that it wasn't just part of me anymore. It became me. It owned me. It was me. And honestly, part of me wondered if I had grown to love it.

"Cindy." Dr. Owens's voice softens.

"What?"

"You should really…brush your hair…before you go back to work."

In that moment, I can tell that she feels sorry for me. That she genuinely believes I am *crazy*. In turn, I feel sorry for *her*. She won't believe me in this moment, not now. She won't see the truth I see. Now I have to go and prove that I'm not crazy.

"Oh, I'm not going back to work," I say. And I walk out the door without a backward glance.

CHAPTER 19

Messages

September 28, 2022, Logan International Airport, Boston

The flight isn't terrible but I can't relax. Feels like I have a blot clot. Could be any second now that I die from a venous embolism. As soon as I land, I veer into a corner and call Dr. Owens.

"I made it to Boston, but I think I have a DVT. I'm gonna go to the ER," I panic into the phone, looking around to make sure nobody is following me.

"Cindy, are you breathing okay?"

"My watch says my O2 sat is 98 percent, but I don't feel right. My chest is tight."

I hang up and slowly make my way to the curb, where it feels like I'm watching myself from outside my body. I look around as I wait for the rideshare to pick me up.

Something about this airport feels so eerie—it's crowded but has this mystic vibe like it's filled with thousands of ghosts, watching me. And the security cameras everywhere. Why are they all pointed at me?

Messages

Is this paranoia or instinct? I don't know which voice to trust. But I need to get out of here.

* * *

September 28, 2022, Boston Hospital, Massachusetts

The ER gleams like a pristine sanctuary: sleek white walls, towering windows, and immaculate floors. The air carries the crisp scent of alcohol swabs, a stark contrast to the familiar, musty odor of Main Hospital. A friendly nurse greets me with a warm smile, her voice a soothing balm to my frayed nerves. She leads me to a spacious waiting room, its emptiness a stark contrast to the overflowing chaos I'm accustomed to.

Where are the patients? Where am I? This place probably only takes private insurance.

After only five minutes, I'm ushered to the back. I don't dare mention what I do for a living, nor do they ask. It's a relief to be treated like a normal person for once, in a place that doesn't have access to my medical history. I can slip away from the stigma of my mental illness, and they can do their jobs. The nurse explains what EKG leads do as she places them onto my chest and hooks them up to the machine. She takes my blood pressure, informing me of my vital signs. Another nurse starts an IV and tells me they are going to draw labs. It's almost fun to act like I have no idea what any of it means.

I describe the signs and symptoms of classic textbook deep vein thrombosis: a hard time breathing, a long plane ride, progressive sensations of chest tightness. And some calf pain, just a little. I genuinely think I'm dying…but somehow, I'm starting to feel slightly relieved, just being here in this hospital—a nice one—where it seems people actually care. *Maybe I will get my cancer diagnosis here. Maybe they have good cancer doctors. If I'm lucky…maybe I'll never have to go back to Main Hospital. At this point, I'd risk my life to stay away from there.*

Nobody can fault me for needing to know if I have leukemia or lymphoma. The hospital I work at is out to get me. They'd rather I was dead. I know what I saw on the ultrasound. I can still feel the lumps in my neck.

The doctor finally arrives, after four hours of labs, waiting, and a chest x-ray. I'm ready. He's here to tell me it's cancer. There's nothing they can do. But it's fine. At least I'm in Boston. At least I can sign up for a clinical trial. I never have to go back to Hawaii. I can enroll somewhere here. Harvard. NIH. Something. A fantasy future plays out in my head.

The doctor greets me with his smile. He asks me what's going on and as tempted as I am to tell him I think I am dying from cancer, I don't want him to think I am insane, so I say, "I'm worried…that I can't breathe…just got off a long flight…"

I can't even say that I think I have a DVT because I realize how fucking stupid and crazy that actually sounds.

Thankfully, he put it together himself. He tells me he ordered a D-Dimer and it's negative. I ask him to feel my neck. He says he ordered a Covid test, too, and it was negative. But I don't have f*cking Covid! I have cancer. But he says there're no lumps in my neck and my chest x-ray is normal. Everything is normal.

Normal? Is he f*cking serious. A state-of-the-art hospital and everything is *normal?*

"I'm just having a hard time breathing…my back…"

"We ordered liver and pancreatic enzymes and those are normal too."

I didn't even consider pancreatitis or liver damage. Good call. Okay, that is reassuring, but still. No cancer? Now, I *am* a bit concerned. Have I really lost my mind?

"Everything is normal," he repeats. "Follow up with your PCM when you get home. Why are you here in Boston?"

"I'm sorry?"

"What is the reason for your trip?"

No way in hell am I telling him I'm a doctor. "I'm here for a writing conference."

"Oh, that's nice." He finishes charting on the computer. "Enjoy your trip and, if anything changes, don't hesitate to come back."

"Okay." I smile as the nurse removes the IV, hands over discharge paperwork, and sends me on my way.

Maybe he can't tell me I have cancer…like, I need to follow up and find out from my PCM. But what about the lumps in my neck? What about the spots on the ultrasound?

TOO MUCH

It is already 11 p.m. and I have to wake up at 5 a.m. for this two-day trauma conference. Then get back on the plane and take call forty-eight hours later in Hawaii.

Regardless, I am on a mission to get to the bottom of this.

I know *this* is something.

* * *

October 2, 2022, Pacific Ocean

I download my chest x-ray from the hospital app before takeoff and stare at it for the majority of the flight. I can only hope the passengers next to me think I'm a budding radiologist, instead of some schizophrenic, paranoid, delusional hypochondriac. I text the image to several of my med school friends, who all assure me it's normal.

Texted Paul, but he says it's normal. I would think by now, of all people, he'd have the balls to tell me I'm dying. That in three months, I'll be dead, so it's perfectly acceptable if I book some random ticket across the world and live my own weird version of *Eat, Pray, Love*. Die in the middle of an epic bucket list adventure.

* * *

October 3, 2022, Main Hospital, Hawaii

Dr. Bates and Dr. Pratt sit in their Herman Miller chairs, silhouetted against the stark white wall. I'm slumped across from them on Dr. Bates's fake leather daybed.

Messages

Dr. Bates hands me the packet—the hefty stack of papers I've been dreading all these years. Before he says the words, I know what this is: termination.

Both of them smile as I take the papers, like they are proud to finally be rid of me. With his pot belly sticking out over his faded scrubs, Dr. Bates rubs his balding head, and says, "Cindy, the CCC voted."

I look away and shake my head.

"You didn't meet the requirements to pass probation."

I don't know what to say.

Dr. Pratt is just the sidekick, the "ENT Assistant Program Director." Together, they're two pot-bellied, balding peas in a pod. "Cindy," she chimes in, "we were disappointed to get this complaint last week."

Dr. Bates flashes a different stack of papers with text messages from my co-residents:

WILL YOU WON'T FUCKING BELIEVE THI—
ARE YOU FUCKING KIDDING ME

It's the messages I sent to the entire residency group chat on accident—I meant to send them to Will. Not to the entire group, but I don't want to start explaining myself. Because I am who I am, I attempt to explain. "This is about that? Are you serious? Because of the text messages? Those texts were about Charli not wanting to take call. Remember New Year's Eve when she had a breakdown and we had to cover for her? How about all those times when Will, Tony, and I took primary call as senior residents to help—I accidentally sent the wrong text to the wrong group."

"Why do you even have a group chat talking about the junior residents like this? How do you think that makes them feel?" Dr. Bates asks.

"What do you want me to do?"

"Stop being unprofessional!" he yells.

"I didn't sign up for this." I break.

"Yes. Yes, you did. We all signed up for this."

I can't fight any longer. I take the termination paperwork, and I decide that it's actually...*a relief.*

Finally. Finally, after all these years. I have nothing to say. Other than: "I need to leave."

Everything inside me. Tells me: *Just leave, Cindy...Just go. Leave. Run.*

Never. Look. Back.

So, I listen.

I reach down into my scrub pocket, find my keys, stick them between my knuckles, turn the doorknob, and slowly exit the room. Leave my two male superiors to watch me go.

After the door clicks shut, I run down the fire exit through the parking lot to my car, unscrew my Addfocus bottle and snort a bump of powder.

My car starts and I'm gone.

* * *

October 2022, Main Hospital Parking Lot, Hawaii

I pull back into the parking lot after realizing why all of this may be happening. It was a text. A text message from a year ago, or maybe two. I can't remember everything I wrote but the gist of it hits me. *I didn't mean anything by it.*

I texted Paul something about how I could, COULD imagine why someone *could* be so angry at their co-workers that they would want to shoot people. But I would never want to do anything.

It all hits me at once.

Is this why?

A huge conspiracy against me?

I don't even own weapons. I would never hurt anyone.

I'm sweating and my car battery is at 11%.

In a panic I step out of the car and sit on the curb, still in my scrubs, my hospital ID badge around my neck. I walk to another curb across the lot, clutching my backpack.

TOO MUCH

I flip open my second phone and call Bradley Brown.

Pick up pick up pick up. Please pick up.

"Cindy?"

"Brad!? Thank God. You won't believe what's happening Brad. This is all a big misunderstanding. They want to terminate me and I think I know why. I think they found out about a text. They think I'm drinking at work—they think I'm I'm—I know I'm on Addfocus and I'll stop but listen—they're after me Brad."

"Who is? Where are you?"

I see a few patients walk by and I lower my voice, get up and walk to the bus stop around the corner.

"Brad," I whisper into the phone. "I think the government…I think they're following me or something—I think they're trying to kill me."

"Cindy, if that's what you really think. I think you need to go to the ER…"

I start bawling. It's the middle of the day. And I have no idea who to trust. What is real. What is a lie. What is happening.

"Okay." I hang up the phone and walk back to my car. SUVs inch towards me and people, all kinds of people seem to creep up around out of nowhere. Men with glasses. Women in scrubs. People lurking around the corner. A yellow school bus honks the horn out of nowhere and I'm startled. It's like I can't breathe. It's like a scene from a horror movie, except I'm the villain. Somehow, I look around and I'm stranded in the middle of the quad and I look up and the American Flag is at half-mast right above me. Is this a conspiracy? It's because of the texts. The emails. The flirting. The innocent, innocent flirting. Maybe it was because of Paul. Because of Brad. Or *was it because of Dr. Thatcher—maybe he reported me to Dr. Bates and Dr. Pratt?*

What if those things inside me aren't lymph nodes? What if I'm being surveilled by some disgusting high-tech Army thing. Like some sick, sick, science project?

Next thing I know, I'm driving way above the speed limit because there's at least 3 or 4 SUVs following me. Honestly. I think it's the FBI. *Why?* When I get to Side's and pull into the lot, the dark SUV that has been on me is nowhere to be seen. But it still feels like I'm not alone.

This is a total set-up.

I've been utterly betrayed. By everyone. Paul, my mom, my coworkers, my own psychiatrist. I walk up to the nurse manning the ER check-in station, and she asks about my reason for visiting.

"I'm having a psychotic episode," I admit.

She blinks, as if she can't believe I'd be so frank, so diagnostic.

"I also work here—sometimes…so if it's possible, I'd like to keep this private." I flash her my ID to show my hospital privileges. Part of me cares. Part of me doesn't. Most of me is no longer ashamed. All of me just wants the truth now.

TOO MUCH

What more do I have to lose? The people I work with think I am a terrorist, after all. That, or I have finally lost my mind.

At this point, I don't know which scenario is worse: Them believing that I'm a full-blown psychopathic terrorist, or that this scenario seems perfectly reasonable.

I need help figuring it out, because I don't seem able to differentiate delusion from reality.

Would I rather be totally insane? Or would I rather be right? The fucked-up part is...I almost would rather be right. That would mean I actually won *something*. Anything. Even one point. That they conspired against me. Because if I lose everything else, at least I can win an argument. So what if it's at the expense of my sanity?

The nurse ushers me into a small section in the ER, next to a desk. It's not a patient room.

"We don't have any beds right now, and the psychiatrist is seeing a few patients," she tells me apologetically, "but we will get them over here as soon as possible."

The nurse two desks over keeps looking at me, and I intentionally empty everything out of my purse to show that I don't have any weapons. There is whispering and giggling all around me. Next thing I know, another nurse guides me into a glass room with a locked door and hands me a blanket, crackers, and water.

"The psychiatrist will be in shortly," she says.

Messages

A petite Asian woman, slender and pretty, walks in next. She looks about my age. I realize I'm judging her based on her appearance, which is exactly what I've been rallying against this whole time. She smiles at me and seems friendly. Nice.

Now I get it. The smile works. It really does. She's playing the game, but look at her, she's a psychiatric resident in the ER, and I'm...crazy?

Somehow, this revelation—here and now—makes me feel all the shittier. *But she's a fucking psychiatrist. Her job is to make people feel better. Is mine?*

I explain the entire day and ask what she thinks about admitting me to the psychiatric ward. "My residency program is out to get me. I'm being followed. Although I'm convinced, I can see everything clearly, I also can't trust what I'm seeing. That's why I am here at Side's. So there would be no bias against me, like there is at Main Hospital. I need help," I finally tell her.

"Is there a family member that you can stay with? We can admit you if you really, really want...but honestly, you won't like it here. It's not nice." She looks at me with pleading eyes, almost as if she is signaling something. Something she isn't allowed to say, in case someone is listening. Like...the idea that this place isn't safe, either.

I look at her with understanding. This hospital has been infiltrated, too. I always suspected it, but now I feel like I have proof.

I'm extremely fucked.

Maybe that's why I was pulled from this place as an intern and never got to return.

The attending walks in, a burly older man, wearing suspenders, a peculiar type. He asks me about my history, and then we realize that we crossed paths in our past lives. He opened up the psychiatric center for adolescents here on the island. I don't remember him, of course, and he really doesn't remember me, but we cross-reference the dates.

"I was fourteen years old when I tried to kill myself," I admit.

"You had to have been my patient," he says. "I was the director of that ward."

But that time wasn't like this. That time I was *just* angry at my mom and truly thought that getting off the planet was the solution. I didn't understand the magnitude of what I had tried to do, and I didn't understand death. I was a teenager. This time is different. This time...I don't actually want to die. I just don't have anywhere else to go, and I want to stop existing *like this*—whatever *this* is.

I want to live. More than anything. I just don't know if I can, because there's nothing and nobody that I trust. He offers me anti-psychotic pills and tells me that it's not safe for me to be around patients or return to work as a doctor until I'm cleared by my psychiatrist back at Main Hospital: Dr. Owens.

We all agree to this plan, and I'm discharged home. Feeling empty and defeated, I go to my mother's house. Lay down on my childhood

Messages

bed, take the anti-psychotic and catch my mom glancing at me through the door. I close my eyes to pretend I'm asleep.

She doesn't ask me what's going on, and I don't tell her.

CHAPTER 20

Egos

November 2022, Hawaii

I'm on a DIY anti-psychosis adventure of *weaning off the wrong pills to get on the right stuff.* A week ago, I was drinking alone at a bar and got invited for more drinks at this guy's place. Flint's his name. A little older, scruffy, not my type. Says he visits from time to time for work and he's off for a few weeks. Says he's staying in a friend's apartment in town. Bunch of people passing around coke and this new thing, k-mine. New to me anyways.

New friends. They accept me for who I really am. It's all kind of a blur and I try k-mine for the first time. They tell me that technically, I can't die from this stuff. Not to do too much coke—I'm a little too f*cked up to remember the physiology but that sounds about right.

The k-mine burns the back of my throat at first and then I'm in a whole new world. The night cascades on. Nothing like karaoke or college.

The base is thumping so loud. Flint makes me another bump. His arm is wrapped around me like I'm already his girlfriend but I don't mind. He's giving me all these drugs for free. This stuff is smooth. It's got this effect I can't quite explain very well—like I'm floating, escaping and nothing matters anymore. This whole world we live in,

Egos

it's gone. It means nothing. My problems have evaporated. I love it and I want more. It feels like another dimension. We're having epic conversations about our existence and we've transcended into a multiverse. Flint looks like a shapeshifting hologram.

He's talking but I can't really make out what he's saying and he starts kissing me. It's not the best, but I don't mind. Next thing I know—his apartment is a pirate ship and the air is so cool and breezy and light and we are laughing and he turns on these LED flashing lights and we dance all night and the morning sun comes up.

I'm puking now. Flint says I'm in a K-hole. He's trying to feed me honey with a spoon from a jar—says that the sugar counteracts the k-mine.

"Open your mouth, you need honey," he insists, holding a spoon of honey to my lips. I can't really think straight but I slowly open my lips and feel the thick honey. Sweet and sticky on my tongue.

I can't really think about the science but all of a sudden, we are back on planet Earth and I'm only seeing one of him. The sugar thing doesn't make sense but I don't feel like talking science. Now I'm in his bed. Somehow, undressed. I don't mind.

Mattress on the floor. Scattered shoes and beer cans crowd the corner of the dirty tile. Reminds me of a place I'd never normally be. Doesn't matter. I'm a nobody. I kind of like it. He asks if I want to go to a bar or club. Or do more K—Flint says to call it "Kitty Kat." I smile because I love secrets and code language.

We get high for another 72 hours. It's a rip-roaring adventure of snorting coke, then Kitty Kat, and back again through it. Phone has zero notifications. Nobody cares.

Screen is blurry at times. I can barely see the words on it—not sure why it's all fuzzy but I can still see Flint. Looks like Gracie texted. Takes me about 10 solid minutes to read her message and I text her that I'm fine—I hope that's what just happened.

My phone dies at some point and it's all kind of funny. We laugh and eat our meals from the gas station. Flint pees in a park and we cuddle and it's fun. We end up at his friend's beach house a couple days after that. We've been vaping and I know it's bad for me, but I like it.

"Do you have to go to work tomorrow?" he asks.

"Oh, no. I'm—it's complicated." I shift my eyes away. Hoping he's not onto me. I sneak some of my pills when I think he isn't looking.

"What are you taking?" He walks over to snoop at what I'm doing, in a gentle way—Flint is kind. Can't stop vaping.

"Just my anti-depressant."

"You can't be mixing pills and this stuff. It's dangerous," he whispers into my ear, caressing my neck.

"Okay," I nod.

Later on we're making out again. He's a smooth talker. Love bombs me all night.

Egos

He asks, "Hey, what's the most messed up thing you ever done?"

"Why?"

He laughs. "Just tell me."

"Um—I don't know. This? I guess." I smile. He doesn't know I'm a doctor—not that it matters in this situation anyway. But—I feel like what I'm doing is okay…I tell myself it is. At his friend's vacant beach house, there's an oversized pool facing the ocean. Calm and serene with the palm trees gently swaying above us. Nobody else wants to swim.

"Be careful," Flint says from the bedroom across the open courtyard.

I don't care about anything. The sun has set and it's getting darker. Looks like some flashing lights above me. Something, somewhere out there tells me to slow down. To stop doing too much. I get out of the pool because it's kind of freezing. And I'm just wearing my underwear.

He's inside with his friends playing music. I'm so high I can't even move my fingers anymore. Find a soft couch on the open yard and stare at the blinking lights. Maybe they are UFOs…or government spies. Hard to say. Or I'm hallucinating…getting sleepy.

Getting these telepathic messages from the sky above me. I think it's the blinking lights. Messages beaming down. They telepathically ask—"Cindy, are you ready to die?" I know it sounds crazy, but these lights, I'm getting telepathic communications from these things in the sky, they're somehow beaming messages down to me, asking if I really want to die right now.

TOO MUCH

It says it will take me. I close my eyes and my heartbeat slows down.

I think I'm ready but—no. Take a hit of the vape.

Not yet, I say telepathically to the sky. I open my eyes and beam back a message: "Let me stay a little longer. I still have shit to do on this planet."

* * *

December 2022, Hawaii

Flint and I have been partying off and on for a few weeks now. But we get into a screaming argument and I spend an hour looking for a piece of jewelry on the ground. Burst into tears crying because it was a gift from my father. In that moment, it's the only thing left that I care about in the world. I'm high but I'm down. On drugs but totally lucid because I realize I have nothing left at all. Nothing in the world. It's all gone. Everything. And then the little diamond stud is there, in a little crevice and I think I might be okay. I decide it's time to go home, to my mom's the next morning. Buy my own vapes at a shop. Can't believe these things cost twenty bucks.

It's the last time we ever see each other—me and Flint—honestly, that's probably not his real name, but whatever he is, wherever he is…I hope he's okay.

* * *

Egos

Been doom scrolling. Reading about Ukraine and Russia. Trying not to think about how it all ties together with the theories in my diary hidden in my nightstand. Our government has its own social media page—*fascinating. Maybe I should post a peaceful protest of my own. Might be a little controversial but at least it's creative.* Change into a white lace halter top and black combat boots. Cherry red lipstick with a pop of plumping gloss. Iconic.

Simulated mortars and gunfire boom through the wall from Kyle's video games. For special effects, I'll take this outside and post my video in the graveled, unfinished section of the house. I know—show the view to my "followers" in the background. *Genius. It's all related.* Screenshot pics of past wars and talk about how war is bad—what an epic demonstration! Boom. Posted. Kind of avant-garde if you ask me.

Go back inside and lay down. Pop a pill. Not sure why all these people are sending me messages. Gracie is blowing up my phone. And now Jennifer—funny how she always drops off when she's dating some guy. Now she suddenly cares about me because I'm dressed like I'm going out?

Ignore.

It's a peaceful protest. Why do they care so much? It's just the war. I mean, not *just*—just me talking about it. I'm a nobody.

Everything feels like a warm blanket. Nice and cozy. I shuffle around and look for the crusty journal I keep in my childhood bedroom, stuffed with small notes my dad gave me years ago, when I was in college. My phone won't stop vibrating. It's Gracie. She won't stop texting.

Cindy, PLEASE delete your posts!

I start scribbling into my journal, a small note to myself about time travel. All of a sudden, I hear Kyle yelling.

"Cindy! Cindy! Your friend is here," he yells.

Confused, I stumble down the hallway. Jennifer barges through the front door like she owns the place, but she's never been here before. She violently grabs my phone from my hands, then snatches away my purse and keys.

"Get the fuck out of my house, I'm not on anything." I reach for my things.

"You need to go to the psych ward, Cindy!" she insists.

I'm so disoriented that I don't question how she knows my mom's address. How she got here so quickly. "Get the fuck off me! Give me my phone!"

"No, Cindy. You are posting crazy shit! You can't talk about the war. Delete it!"

"I did! I was just texting Gracie. Fuck off! What are you doing here?"

"I'm here because I love you!" Jennifer pleads with her eyes doe-wide.

Egos

This reasoning doesn't make any sense to me in my frame of mind. She loves me? Why is she yelling at me and threatening me? That isn't love. "Get the fuck out of my house!"

"Cindy?" Kyle appears from the hallway.

"Kyle, tell this girl to get out of my house! Call Mom! Call the cops right now."

"Cindy, you are on drugs!" Jennifer says and retreats with my phone to the corner of the kitchen. Time seems to blur and speed along.

"Cindy, the cops are here," Kyle says as he looks out the window curtains.

"Are you fucking serious?" I say, following him to double-check. I don't know if these are cops that Jennifer called *about* me, or Kyle called *for* me. Are they here to hurt me or to help me?

"Cindy, talk to Paul." Jennifer waves the phone to my face.

"Oh, fuck you, Jen!" I yell.

"Cindy. Cindy. They are going to involuntarily admit you," Paul says.

"Paul. Are you fucking serious right now? Why? Because I posted some dumb shit that makes no sense?" I say into the phone, watching the cops getting out of their cars, hot tears streaming down my face.

"Cindy, you are on the wrong meds and everyone is worried," Paul says.

"Who the fuck is worried? I'm not suicidal or homicidal. I know the law. Are *you all* the *insane* ones?" I look at Jennifer and my brother.

"Cindy, are you suicidal?" Paul asks.

"Paul, I just said I wasn't. Listen to yourselves. You are all fucking monsters. You know what? I wish I could. I fucking *wish* I had the balls to kill myself but I fucking don't, and you know why?"

"Cindy, you know I lost some of my best friends after we redeployed—I lost them to suicide," Paul is saying. "Just so you know, you do that—you do that—that's the most selfish thing you could ever do! You do that and you kill your family, Cindy. You think about that when you're in the psych ward."

My entire body is full of rage. I could destroy all of them. "I know that, *Paul*. You wouldn't even let me finish!"

Jennifer throws her hands up. "He's just saying—"

"No, what *I was just saying* is that I can't kill myself because of *you fucking people*." I clap my hands on each syllable for emphasis but my body feels comfortably numb, disconnected. "I don't kill myself so that it doesn't hurt you, and this is how you treat me? Fuck off. *Fuck all of you!*" I scream at the top of my lungs and storm back into my childhood bedroom.

Ironic that just a month ago, I was the one fighting to get a ticket into the psych ward, but now, here, with others pleading for me to go, that's the last place I want to be.

Egos

This is my nature, I suppose.

My downfall.

Jennifer gets on the phone with Dr. Owens.

Lynn walks in. Of all things.

"Mom!" Kyle rushes over to Lynn and gives her a hug like he's the victim. "Mom," he continues, his voice cracking with fear, "Cindy put an ax in the hallway closet!" He points a shaking finger at me, his eyes wide with fear.

"No, I didn't!" I scream at Kyle, my voice thick with fury. Hot tears well up in my eyes.

"Yes, you did, Cindy! I saw you!" My mom rushes to the hallway closet and reveals the ax from our garden shoved into the corner.

"Mom, I just put it there, just in case!" I sob, my voice barely a whisper. I glance back at the cops in the hallway, their presence suffocating. Jennifer stands behind them, her eyes cold and accusing. My heart pounds in my chest, a trapped bird.

"Cindy, you're acting crazy," my mother whispers.

A laugh bubbles up, bitter and raw. "You know what? I am crazy! So what? What are you people going to do about me? That's right! I'm fucking PSYCHO! Big deal? And—so was my dad! You gave him such a hard time about it, mom! Are you going to give me a hard time about it, too?"

TOO MUCH

"Officer, I'm sorry, I can't be here." Mom retreats to her bedroom, her sobs echoing down the hallway. Kyle follows, leaving me alone with the cops and Jennifer, frozen in the corner, clinging to her purse like a shield, her eyes avoiding mine.

The cops surround me, their questions a meaningless drone. They bark at me, their voices harsh and accusatory. I feel like a specimen under a microscope, my every word dissected and analyzed. Am I a doctor? Am I in the military? Am I crazy? My head spins. I don't know what's real anymore. Too discombobulated to call my lawyers.

Before I know it, cold steel clamps around my wrists. I'm being escorted to the back of a car. Cuffed in the back of a cop car because one of my best friends called about my unhinged social media posts. In shock, all I can do is resort to the one thing I've known my entire life to get me through: dark humor. And I crack a joke with the cop to break the awkward silence.

"I've never been in the back of a cop car before—I mean, it wasn't on my bucket list. But at least—at least I can say I've done it—so you know—crossing it off my bucket list now."

He doesn't laugh too loud but I feel like he's smiling inside. I think he feels bad for me. Pretty sure he's been to my mom's house before. Pretty sure they legitimately think I'm crazy. I know it's dumb to crack a joke about getting cuffed in a time like this and I seem crazy, but it's the only way I can cope. It's a pretty fucked situation. The metal rubs against my wrists. The cold seats are uncomfortable. The partition between me and their faces—all I did was post something online—right?

Egos

I tell myself that maybe it's for the best. Maybe this is Jennifer's way of showing me her love, after all. It's not until later that I wonder why everyone's version of love for me equals pain, coercion, control.

* * *

January 2023, Psychiatric Inpatient Clinic, Hawaii

"Dr. Owens is on the phone, Cindy."

I race to the phone. Wish I had the vape with me.

"Dr. Owens—hi. Are you coming to see me? They are stating I was going to kill people—you have to believe me—it's not true. But listen. I wrote a resignation letter. Just with a pen and paper that they gave me here, but I was wondering if you can give it to Dr. Bates for me?"

"Cindy, I can't be your psychiatrist in the ward. But I'm happy to have an appointment scheduled as soon as your doctor thinks it's okay for you to be discharged."

"Do you know anything about my plan? My meds? I hope you don't think anything less of me. I'm sorry about what I said to you—for the yelling."

"I understand, Cindy. I'm just glad you are okay. Please focus on your health. We don't want anyone writing resignation letters in the ward."

We hang up the phone. Losing Dr. Owens at the same time I lost the program just after losing Brad felt like losing Paul and my father all over again. Like I didn't really have anything at all. A dream and a nightmare all in one.

The psych ward is driving me a bit bonkers after 24 hours. Prison beige uniform. The bland food. Staring at the ceiling. Having to borrow a pen. Not having a TV or a cell phone. Staring out the window and wondering if the flashing lights really are aliens.

Not saying this for shock factor but I'm kind of a disgusting person.

Life is not an all-you-can-eat buffet. I had to cut my losses. Looking back at it all, the hardest thing I've ever had to do? Hands down, say no to drugs. It wasn't passing my Organic Chemistry class. It wasn't standing like a statue for hours on end in an OR. It wasn't pretending to be dumb or staying up all night studying or training for the Army fitness l tests I barely passed. For me, the hardest thing I ever had to do, was choosing to say no to drugs. This is a daily choice. It is a choice I have to make more than once a day. It's a constant battle.

Because the one thing in the world that can take all the mistakes, the pain, the agony, the sorrow, the depression, the pain, all the fuckery away—is the bliss, the pure high. Does that make a person *bad*? I don't know.

It has to end.

It's killing everyone around me. If I could have it all, I would. I'd do it all. All the time.

But I can't. For the first time, it's too much and I don't want it all. Not anymore—because having it all doesn't actually feel good.

Egos

The next day I'm interviewed by the inpatient team. They're considering discharge—if we can agree on a plan. The lead psychiatrist is a tall
slender man, in glasses. Stereotypical type—not sure why everything
in real life seems like it's from a movie, but it is. There's a female with
him. Another interrogation. They ask me about my entire psychiatric
history. My childhood. Then some unusual questions like why I'm
researching conspiracies. I pretend that I'm not. That I *know nothing*.
I do my best to act like I don't know about the lights in the sky. The
UFOs. Time travel. They ask me if I hear voices. If I see things. Of
course, I say no. I'll do anything to get discharged. What if they keep
me locked up forever because they think I'm schizophrenic? I know
I'm "crazy" but not crazy enough to be *here*. I'm a doctor for crying
out loud. I can take care of myself. I just need meds. I just need to
stop doing drugs. I just need…to be free.

They prescribe me mood stabilizers. We agree that I'll stop taking
stimulants and sedatives. We agree to an outpatient plan. And I agree
to stop posting on social media. When I'm discharged, I go back to
my mom's house and spend the next two weeks there. I spent the last
18 years of my life avoiding that house, resenting that it was unfinished. Vowing that I'd never live in it again. And of all places, it's the
one place I need to be the most.

So many times, I'd scream at my mom to sell the house, to move, to
find something better for herself. She was getting old. Dad was dead.
He would want her to have something better. It didn't really dawn
on me until shuffling up the steps and stopping at the top of them,
to gaze out and realize—they had such a nice view. All of these years,
I was always so fixated on the gravel, the cinderblocks, what wasn't
finished—never bothering to appreciate the untouched glory.

TOO MUCH

* * *

February 2023, Psychiatric Outpatient Clinic

Dr. Kaleo's office space is dark but cozy. There are two wooden chairs and three tall bookcases. Shelves on shelves are filled with jars of tea from all over the world.

"Choose any chair you want," he says.

I sit in the seat closest to the door, settling into the dark, forest-green leather, rubbing my hand along the gold studs on the armrests.

"What is your expectation for this first visit today?" he asks.

"I don't expect a diagnosis, and I don't expect you to have a total understanding of my life story after an hour. Honestly, this is kind of dumb, and I haven't even Googled it to see if it exists, but I came up with an app idea. It's like totally a manic thing, but anyway, really quick, here's my—"

"Stop," he said.

"What?"

"Stop doing that. You see what you are doing there?"

"What?"

"You're probably so used to undermining yourself that you don't even realize it." He takes a deep breath, maintaining eye contact.

Egos

My heart is pounding. How has he caught on so quickly? It's a balancing act to keep my legs from bouncing while I hang onto his every word.

"We call this, what you're doing now, a manifestation of imposter syndrome. You come up with an idea, but—because you are a woman and so used to being around, let me guess, sensitive men with fragile egos—you have to dumb yourself and your ideas down. Make them small and seemingly less intimidating. Eventually, you sabotage yourself so you can fit into this image of not being good enough."

I look at the scribbles on his yellow notepad, and, for the first time, in a long while, I don't know what to say. We haven't even been interacting for three minutes yet. How does he know me this well already? He hasn't heard about my childhood. My suicide attempt. My this, my that. Yet from listening to my haphazard thirty-second introduction to my current state of whatever we want to call *this*, he gets that my problem is not entirely my mental illness.

Maybe the root of my problem isn't *just* me, or my failures, or myself. Maybe what I'm experiencing is very much related to and, in fact, founded upon my environment, past, present, *and everything in between.*

"I don't care about the diagnosis," I insist.

"Oh, but you do." He twirls his pen in his hand.

"No, I just said I don't care."

"That's a negation. By saying you don't care, you're highlighting and bringing attention to the fact that you *do* care. If you didn't care, you wouldn't be focusing on that. You wouldn't even be saying that. But you've mentioned it twice since we've been sitting here."

Where has this person been all my life? Yes, it's intimidating to sit in his office and feel like he sees right through me to my deepest core, but isn't that what I've always wanted? To simply exist? To be seen for myself and not whatever label has been applied to me? Or whatever label I've applied to myself?

At the beginning of my residency program, I resented the idea of being labeled, especially because society attaches such a stigma to mental health issues. Terrified to say anything about my mental health. It didn't seem wise for a budding surgeon to admit having any weaknesses.

Once Paul got to know me, he danced around the topic of me being bipolar. Yes, there were times when I lost my handle on my emotions—like when I ripped that bookshelf out of the wall. When we were married, Paul would only say that I was "*acting* bipolar," but he stopped short of acknowledging me as truly being sick in the DSM sense.

I've struggled.

My mania has made my life a blur. I can't fully remember what medications I've tried. Why they failed or worked. What side effects I experienced. How I recovered. If I recovered at all. In a strange and uncomfortable way, talking to Dr. Kaleo like this actually feels good. He is giving me something the residency program never has. Validation. Honesty. Maybe even…acceptance.

Egos

Truth.

"What I mean is, I want to change it. I don't want people to focus on my label or diagnosis, like bipolar, or whatever. I don't want people to feel embarrassed or ashamed for having a mental illness. *Everyone* has a degree of mental illness."

I see it in my patients. In people's medical histories. Their prescription lists. A lot of people walk around pretending, but self-medicating with alcohol and popping pills on the side.

"*You see?* You want to change it. You care." He points his pen at me.

"Do you think the government is following me...I mean...I can see why there'd be concerns?"

"Why would there be concerns?" He shifts again in his chair.

"I moved to the beach – sold my condo. And a lot of my designer handbags. And...bought a new car? I think – I was going through a phase. I don't know if that's mania. Depression. But honestly, I think people here think I'm a terrorist. And I feel like people are following me."

"Nobody thinks you're a terrorist. Are you out buying fertilizer?"

"No."

"Well, why would you say that?"

I look away. "People don't like me here. I never belonged." And it hit me. One day Tony tried to reassure me that he didn't have "skin in the game." That he didn't care. Was that just a negation statement. Was I right about him all along? Or was I really crazy? I'll never really know the truth. It was too late. And part of me was truly too tired to care. At least about Tony. And whatever it was that he had or hadn't done to play a hand in getting me to where I landed.

Dr. Kaleo completes the assessment and initiates my medical discharge paperwork from the United States military. He diagnoses me with acute psychosis. Walking out of the office, I step into my new car and coast along the freeway, driving across the island in a car I really can't afford—I bought in a state of absolute mania. I think back to when I thought people in the government were legitimately following me and check my rear-view mirror.

It's possible that I'm being followed and I'll just have to live with it, if it's true. I'll never know. I can't prove it didn't happen and I can't prove that it did. I need to move on. For now, the only solace I find is in being alone. Spending my days and nights inside an apartment tucked way far away from the city, away from the hospital, away from the life I built and the people I loved so very dearly. Trying to forget everything that nearly killed me.

People don't like me. But maybe I don't belong in that box of a hospital. Is it because I asked too many questions? Because I wanted to come up with solutions? And that was not allowed? Was it because I searched for truths that nobody could fix?

This meant I was a threat to a system that was intended to protect and help people, but inadvertently harming us—all of us. Maybe I *was* a terrorist in that regard.

Egos

I realize that the way we react to others is a reflection of what exists within us, a reflection of how we outwardly see the world and inwardly see ourselves.

I do still care. Deeply. And caring too much torments me. In everything I do. Everywhere I go. In every relationship I have. I cared for my patients. For my friends. For my colleagues. Even the ones who seemed to hate me. For Kyle, for my parents. For everything they had gone through and sacrificed to set me up for success.

Nobody is a dead-end. Even if they left. I'm still here. I can't help it. I tried to leave. I tried to die. So many times. In so many ways. But in the last moment. In the last second. I couldn't.

I care to make a bigger difference in the world and build a life for myself that I can be proud of. I cared for my dad too much to let him live the rest of his life in the ICU, attached to machines and undergoing dialysis when he couldn't even walk on his own two legs. I still care for Paul. Even long after he moved out and we got divorced, I care that he goes on to live a happy and healthy life, and discover the true meaning of love and peace.

I care about all of this, after all. And I'm not sorry.

I care enough to go up against the cheating, corruption, and systemic inequality in my residency program and the institution that protects it. I care, and caring almost broke me—weathering my mind, body, and soul. To the point that I had gone from trying to convince one set of ER doctors to admit me to trying to convince another set of psych doctors that it was *them* and not me, who was crazy, unable to sift delusion from reality.

TOO MUCH

So what if I am crazy, like my dad? So what if I am different? I was asked to be someone else, to care less and smile more. If that's the worst that people can say about me—that I'm crazy, psycho, delusional—so what?

I pull over at the convenience store and buy boxed bleach to dye my hair. I'll take some epic selfies but post them under a fake name so people don't flip out. A homeless lady sitting on the curb asks me for change.

"Sorry, I don't carry cash." It's the truth. If I did, I would have spared some. Get back in my car and cruise along the coast with the windows down. Middle of the day, no traffic. Scattered tents line pockets of the shoreline. Decide it's time for radical change. Like Tony suggested.

Stop off at another small urban oasis and rack up my credit card at the hardware store. I deserve solitude. Peace. Quiet. Freedom. A new life.

Buy a burner phone. Survivor stuff. Emergency batteries. Flashlights. Maybe I'll try camping in the woods. Thank God for all those post-apocalyptic shows I watched. And of course, all that surgical training. I don't need anyone. I'll live alone for the rest of my life.

Maybe if I'm banished to a state of isolation, people will just forget about me and I'll forget about them and we can all move on from this tragedy. Maybe I can start over. Somewhere else. Anywhere else. If only I can just learn to be a different person. If only I can change.

CHAPTER 21

Emails

March 2023, North Shore, Hawaii

The government has been keeping tabs on me. Been laying low since the appointment with Dr. Kaleo. My hair is bleach blonde-orange now. My friends barely text back and it's not safe to drive. People on the beach keep staring. Looking out, I can see them staring back at me. Keep pacing around. Checking to make sure I locked the door. Hate when anyone says hello to me. I'm not sure who to trust anymore. Even my neighbors seem suspicious. They could be spies. Questioning if I died that night in the K-hole. At least I quit vaping.

Still preparing for an apocalypse—just in case. Bought more flashlights. Packaged snacks. Had to get a third phone. Pretty sure my other two are tapped. Also, I'm on a roll with my *government conspiracy diary*. Been connecting the dots, like historical events in the news—things I never read in-depth while I was in med school and residency. All that time wasted. A lot of the news doesn't add up when you take the time to make sense of it. A lot of real stuff has been going on in the world. Stuff that matters outside the hospital.

Unsolved murders. That's what I'm really digging into. What else am I supposed to do? They say I'm on indefinite medical leave until I'm discharged from the Army and I can't get a real job and I can't go back to doing drugs. Almost died in a K-hole.

Maybe I can find out who murdered these children. Better than fig-uring out why there's a war happening. Can't get arrested again. I'll go crazy in the psych ward.

* * *

April 2023, Hawaii

One of these unsolved murders really bothers me. I'm obsessed. Days of dirty dishes pile up in the kitchen, but it doesn't matter—nobody is coming to visit. Stale coffee sits on my nightstand. Spend all day and night on websites and forums dedicated to solving the murder. Not going to name names, but if you know, you know. I've been reading the ransom note as if there's some hidden message. Printed it out. Looking up ciphers. Something about the note sounds so famil-iar. Yes, I know a lot of the phrases are from movies but it goes much deeper—like a voice, a familiar voice that I know.

I text Paul. I'm bothered. I'm distraught. I've also been digging into Natasha's murder.

> Paul, are you sure they caught the right guy? Your soldier, Natasha. I'm reading about her.

He texts me back that they got the right guy. I'm losing my mind. I tell myself to stop going down the wrong rabbit hole. I'm confused. I go back to the unsolved murder. The one with the note. I read it again and again. And again. Aloud. Why does it sound like my writing? Maybe it was the movies. Maybe I am fucked up. Maybe I read too many books? What's wrong with me. Maybe I'm psychotic. Maybe I need meds.

Emails

I don't know how to explain it. I've seen this writing before. It sounds like me. What if—no. Multiverse theory. Simulation theory. Fuck. I'm onto something, but every single time I feel like I'm so close to solving this thing, whatever it is we are in, I lose it. I lose the answers. I know. It was a cover-up. A conspiracy.

Something about the note. Something about the note. Something about the note.

It snaps. It's a marker. Why a marker. Why those quotes. Why those words.

That person was a writer. Had to be...*or has to be?*

It's time to call the government out for covering this up. What else do I have to lose at this point?

Make a field trip to the office supply store in town and pick up several packages of bright green duct tape. A stapler. Permanent markers. All different kinds and colors. That will get their attention. The CIA following me. I know they're watching. Take a fresh black marker and caption it "JUSTICE WILL BE SERVED." Make 1000 copies. Next, I'm racing around town like a mad woman, stapling and taping the fliers to every wooden pole I can find. *We'll find the writer. The murderer. The conspirators!*

The tape residue sticks to my skin. Nothing makes sense. Why a writer? How could a writer do something so heinous? How could they? Why was it covered up? Why don't we have answers? Why am I asking this now? Why am I here? Why is this happening to me? Why am I so insane? Why am I losing my mind?

TOO MUCH

A normal looking couple stops me, "Honey, they didn't solve that? Isn't that from years ago?" she says sweetly, with a look of concern.

I shake my head. Not embarrassed about anything these days. "Oh, they're gonna solve it. You'll see."

"Are you related to that girl," her partner adds, with a raised brow.

"Maybe—" this answer startles me. Where is this coming from? *Maybe? Who is they?* I'm livid. I'm shaking. I'm losing my mind. Why permanent ink pens? And I continue on my mission. Stop at the local library, apply for a library card to use the computer. Buy a plane ticket to Vegas. Seems like a good idea. Maybe I can make new friends and start a new life there. Win the lotto. For real this time.

Gracie texts and asks if we are still on for sushi.

A pleasant surprise. Almost forgot I still had a friend.

Outside the sushi place, my company commander is waiting. He's with several cops. Cop cars swarm the entrance. Sabotaged. I can't outrun them.

What is this? How did they find me. All of my posters and fliers and permanent markers, they're stuffed inside my trunk. Oh god. The horror. I hope—they don't search my vehicle. Are they—here for me? Maybe not. Maybe I can just…act normal. For once. Please, Cindy, just act f*ck-ing NORMAL.

The commander walks up to me with two cops. Says that I've been acting erratic.

Emails

"Captain Neighbors, we need to bring you to the hospital. We've gotten a few concerning phone calls. You haven't been responding to our calls or texts. A BOLO was sent out."

I don't say anything. *A BOLO? What crime have I committed?* I fold one of the fliers and hand it to Gracie with a look in my eyes like my life depends on her to save it and never let anyone confiscate it. She has tears in her eyes. I feel so awful that she has to see this—this company commander taking me away—to the psych ward. Again.

I hope they don't go digging through my government conspiracy diary. There's a lot of good stuff in there—even if it's not true. It's still good.

* * *

This time in the psych ward is different. I call Paul to let him know I'm okay. It's a different psych ward and I've been here for a few days— been playing board games. Watching movies like *Girl Interrupted*, when we aren't doing group or individual therapy. Pretty iconic if you ask me. The doctors reassess my meds—I've legitimately been off drugs since December. They adjust my medication, prescribing a different anti-psychotic. I don't disagree. I don't mind being in the hospital this time. The other patients are nice to me. We've been secretly swapping conspiracy theories and trading snacks at lunch time. I have more stuff to add to my diary when I get home. I kind of like the prison beige scrubs now. It's so chic, don't you think? And the rules. I got used to them. I guess. Made friends with the nurses. They're nice to me here. Reminds me of being a kid again, when Dad and I delivered mangoes around town with supplies. Those were the days.

TOO MUCH

When I discharge, they say I need to be in constant communication with my commander—so I don't recklessly post about conspiracies, online or in real life.

At home, I adjust to the new medication. Spend my waking hours researching things other than conspiracies. Now I'm busy researching some laws. Stuff that has to do with residency and the military. I'm realizing maybe some unjust things happened to me. Also, I started writing. On the computer. Not just scribbles in my notepads. Focusing on my health. Trying not to go insane. Staying off social media. Trying not to get involved in new relationships. With each passing day, like the ocean, there's an ebb and flow of emotion.

Some days, I'm on the beach crying over the losses. Other days, I'm in bed.

It's predictably unpredictable.

* * *

May 2023, My Computer

Jennifer's graduating. She's pregnant. Of all things. Snooping her socials from my stalker account. In a month, she's moving off island. I won't get to say goodbye. Another one. Gone. Tony is leaving, too. Not that I care about saying goodbye to him. Can't keep stalking everyone online—Gabis *euro vacay*, Adam's *new baby*, influencers I don't even know scoring free skincare—but I can't help myself. It's driving me insane watching their filtered faces and perfectly curated lives while I sit here, rotting my millennial youth away.

Emails

All of the scenes and conversations leading up to this moment replay over and over in my mind. Same songs on repeat. Sometimes I write down the conversations, thinking it will help. I can remember word for word what some people said—like a movie that won't stop playing. Dr. Bates. Paul. Dr. Owens. Brad. Dr. Thatcher. All of these scenes stuck in my head.

I keep writing, revising, searching... what does it all mean? Screenplays, poems, even a dusty ENT textbook. Could I go back to residency? The thought dies as quickly as it came. Anger surges. I swim until my lungs burn, pace the beach until my feet blister. The sand clings to my skin, a gritty reminder of my solitude. Weeks pass. No voices but my own echoing my tattered apartment.

Review all the comments, the "feedback," and research sham peer-review online. Come across this website about farms and how depressed people are targeted. Learn about gang-stalking and boom I'm in a rabbit hole once again. It's disgusting. Another twisted game…is this what happened to me? *Were my co-workers targeting me?*

I shake the sick thoughts out of my head and pace around again and again. Play with weights. Yoga. Smoothies. Research more laws. Read the constitution. Fire up an email to my lawyers. Haven't talked to them in a while. It's time we make some aggressive moves. Why am I just sitting around, stuck on a beach anyway?

I decide I do want to say goodbye to Tony after all. I'm not invited to the graduation party, of course. I'll send him a fun parting gift—an American flag.

Fuck it. I'll order myself one, too. The occasion? Graduation.

In my mind, I served enough time. Five years at that hell-hole.

Technically, I should have graduated. I order us flags to be flown over the Capitol on the 4th of July. Epic. Best $134 I've ever spent in my entire GD life.

Going to have his shipped to his next hospital so it's there when he arrives.

What a glorious surprise.

* * *

June 2023, North Shore, Hawaii

Can't work outside of this god-forsaken apartment because I'll get arrested for expressing my concerns about unsolved murders and conspiracies. Any wrong move on social media and boom, the cops show up.

Ridiculous. I'll send emails.

What can people do about my emails? Arrest me?

> **Email Draft**
> **To: me.**
> **Subject: limbo land**
> Paul can't help .big conspiracy. But -I persist., going no-where fast. eating away at my soul.

* * *

Emails

July 4th 2023, Hawaii

4th of July is a joke. I'm stuck on the beach. And this isn't freedom. It's a prison. Company commander harassing me. Sending me emails.

Ignore.

Already enough having to deal with the spies on the beach. At least the flags will be flown over the Capitol today.

Commander says there is a warrant for my arrest. Says I am going to be AWOL. I'm not AWOL. Not sure why anyone would say that about me. I'm going to keep writing emails to the National Council. National Board of Otolaryngology…Congress.

Email Draft
To: me
Subject: events
They say I can't doctor, "too crazy surgeon," but where is restitution and the – about the cheating?
Been firing off email after email. Hiring lawyer after lawyer. termination papers. now that it's me vs the Army.
two full rehab stints outpatient rehab
two more emails. congressional leader. ask for intervention. ask the NBO for a letter.
Weeks pass & To my dismay, NBO sends me a letter -----
then like a succession of events – congression…

* * *

281

TOO MUCH

July 10, 2023, North Shore

The ocean beckons, a siren song of escape. I stumble onto the beach, a bottle of wine clutched in my hand. The cool sand squishes between my toes as I drag my boogie board towards the water. The waves crash around me, a symphony of chaos that mirrors the storm raging inside my head. I paddle out, the alcohol warming my veins, numbing the pain of rejection and failure.

"What do you want from me?" I scream at the waves, my voice hoarse and raw. "What else do you want?" I can see flashing lights. In the sky. In the ocean. It's them. They're watching. The same ones I saw the night I was in the K-hole.

What do they want?

The ocean roars back, indifferent to my anguish. I take another swig of wine, trying to silence the voices in my head.

"FUCK YOU!" I cry, tears mixing with the saltwater on my cheeks. "WHAT DO YOU WANT FROM ME?" I cry and lay on the boogie board as the waves keep crashing. The wine sloshes around and eventually into the ocean. Clutching onto the bottle, I wonder if a wave will take me to oblivion. Take me away from this pain.

"Take me away," I sob into the ocean. I dip my body underwater and scream as loud as I can, emptying myself into the belly of the 'āina. Screeching everything I ever had. Everything I ever lost. "Please," I beg, "just tell me what else you want. I have nothing left."

Emails

The ocean won't take me. Not now. Not like this. Defeated. Broken. Empty. Lost.

Suddenly, a strong hand grips my arm, pulling me back towards the shore. I blink, disoriented, and see a concerned face peering down at me. It's Kai, the friendly neighbor from down the hall.

"Are you okay?" he asks, his tone gentle but firm.

"I'm fine," I slur, trying to pull away. "Just leave me alone."

But he doesn't. He helps me onto the beach, his grip firm but not unkind. "Let's get you inside," he says.

I stumble along beside him, my bare feet dragging along the sandy concrete, the world tilting and swaying.

He leads me to my apartment, his bulky arm supporting my weight. As I fumble with the keys, I mumble, "Thank you."

He nods and turns to leave, but then pauses. "Take care of yourself," he says softly.

I nod, too ashamed to meet his gaze. I watch him walk away, the guilt and self-loathing swirling within me like the churning ocean waves.

Before I doze off to sleep, I send an email to my lawyers and company commander.

Email
To: company commander

TOO MUCH

* * *

July 15, 2023

Spend a few days sobering up, locked inside. The floors of my apartment are scattered with sand. The kitchen counters piled up with more dirty dishes, notepads, colored markers, and more tape. Books everywhere—begging to be read. Can't keep living in this state of destitution. I must escape.

Fling open my laptop to send another email. Wifi is down. Try to turn on the light but it seems the electricity isn't working. Phone battery is low. The electric company says that my electricity has been shut off because the bill hasn't been paid and something about the meter and it can't be turned back on for days...am I that behind on life? Open up my bank account on my cell phone to find my checking account is 0.01.

Exactly one penny to my name. Is this a joke?

Call back the electric company and beg them to turn the electricity on since I need the internet. As fate would have it, when I was in my super paranoid-manic state, I bought a portable power station. "Just in case" so I use it for my computer and hop on the hot-spot.

Emails

You guessed it. To send emails. But it's not just any email. I let it rip. I send a full force barrage of emails. Like an attack. I send emails to Congressional leaders.

Copy and paste. I send emails to the NBO. To the NCRA. Create a new social media account just to message doctors and news outlets. As quickly as I can find them in the search bars.

The Army shut off my pay and electricity while I was still enrolled in the residency program? I haven't been terminated—yet. Technically, I'm on medical leave. Hadn't been through the due process of the termination.

That's right. While I recognize I was high as a kite and a bit crazy, after I got sober and out of rehab, did some research and reviewed the laws, the hospital didn't follow protocols and procedures.

I. Let. It. Rip.

I'm talking over 50 emails. I mean, at this point, I don't even have a fridge to keep my food cold—or money to buy food.

Can you blame me?

* * *

July 18, 2023, Hawaii

Electricity is still off and there's knocking at the door. Company commander's been harassing me on emails and I've been emailing back everyone. The command. The NCRA. National Board of Otolaryngology. Congressional leaders. Everyone. Can't get the electric back on. Can't get discharged from the Army. Can't get a job. And no way to get a paycheck without one? Makes no sense. Can't even work anywhere right now if I tried anyway since everyone is spying on me.

I'm sick of this. Sick of this concept that perception is reality. Reality is reality. I was terminated almost a year ago—and a new email says that I falsified my case logs. Main Hospital opened up another investigation against me. I can't be discharged from the Army because of another investigation!?

Now, I'm AWOL: Absent Without Leave. *AWOL without pay and without electricity. What a sick, twisted joke. Can't post fliers or social media if I wanted to have a hobby. No freedom of speech?*

I see the cops at the door. Again with the cops? Always the cops. Why? Don't they have actual criminals in this town to arrest—other than me…? I mean—I'm innocent, aren't I?

I open the door and there's three of them. One is a strikingly beautiful local. Hazel eyes, tall, athletic. Tropical Barbie Cop.

Oh gosh—if I have to play Cindy Barbie, I WILL.

"What's going on?" I pretend like I have no idea what's going on.

"Are you Captain Neighbors."

I want to say no.

"Yes…"

Emails

"The military police out there in the parking lot—they're saying that you're AWOL, ma'am."

"No, no—" I shake my head and leave the door wide open. "Hold on—I have paperwork."

The place is in absolute ruins. Disgusting. Pens, papers, food wrappers. Clothes—dirty and clean strewn about. Sand on the floor.

"Here—this. It's my medical leave of absence paperwork. Right there. Says I'm bipolar."

I'm almost proud to be crazy. Happy. Gloating almost—to be crazy. Of all things, of all sinister things—it's my "get out of jail card."

Barbie Cop talks into her radio. "Ma'am, we'll be back."

I close the door just enough to see the officers in their dark uniforms, huddling in the parking lot like a swarm of bees. Goodness—there's probably ten people total in the parking lot. What did I do? I sent emails. EMAILS. Half of them make no sense. I'm just asking for my discharge papers. My electricity was shut off. My paycheck. It's not too much to ask for basic things.

"Ma'am, they say you have a lawyer?"

"Uh. I did—"

"You need to get in touch with your lawyer." She hands me my paperwork back. "And the JAG will be in touch with them." They start walking away as another call dispatches to their radio.

TOO MUCH

"That's it?"

"Have a good day, ma'am."

Barbie Cop walks away. I wanted to tell her that she's pretty, but I don't. Is that bad?

The next day, I figure out the lawyer situation as I'm assigned Trial Defense Counsel or as they call it, TDS, in the military. They explain to me that a federal warrant was put out for my arrest because I hadn't checked in with my company commander like I was ordered to, which is why my paycheck was shut off.

The phone call is a blur. They say I need to physically meet with them at a local coffee shop and bring documents and sign a document. They tell me I could go to jail. I tell them I'm only meeting with them if my mom can come because it's not safe. When I call my mom, I make sure to explain to her the gravity of the situation because after all, I could go to jail and we don't want Lynn messing everything up.

* * *

August, 2023, Coffee Shop, Hawaii

My mom and I pull up to the coffee shop and park outside.

"Mom, just try not to say anything—"

"I'm not, Cindy."

"This whole situation is really f*cked."

Emails

"Do you have to curse, Anak."

"Sorry, mom, this is stressful." I reach over the console for a hug, tears spilling over. Two females approach a table outside the shop and sit down with a folder. Dressed in civilian clothing. "I think that's them. Let's go. Let's not give them any information, mom. Remember, even though they say they are my lawyers—they work for the government. The government that is trying to put me in jail." I try not to raise my voice but can't help myself.

"Okay, Anak." She lowers her eyes and her arm is shaking as she opens the car door, barely able to figure it out. I reach over to help her push the button and can't stop myself from bawling in her arms. She hugs me for a quick moment before I gather myself to meet these Army spies.

My mom and I sit and listen to the attorneys explain the serious nature of the federal warrant. How they will try to have it removed and they present me with a counseling form to sign. In exchange, I flash them a stack of papers. It's my medical documentation.

"Is this because I filed a Congressional Inquiry?"

"No, your company commander says you haven't met the requirements to check in for reporting."

"What requirements?"

"He says he's been trying to get in contact with you? You're not answering your phone or email?"

"I'm trying to get my medical discharge paperwork. Also—" I lower my voice. "I'm a protected Whistleblower."

"Any information you can provide to us, that would be helpful for your case. Right now, you're facing a Board of Inquiry. Administrative Separation from the Army."

I shake my head and look at my mom.

"My daughter, she's very sick."

"We understand. What we can do to help—we are asking for documentation so we can help build your daughter's defense case."

"What defense case?" I thought that you said the warrant is dropped?" my mother asks.

"We are going to work on that today. Hopefully—she doesn't have to go in for processing charges for that—"

"Well, there is a new case they just opened up," the older lawyer with a Southern twang wearing sunglasses interrupts her. "And she may have to do a Board of Inquiry—if the medical discharge isn't approved. We don't know yet." She offers my mom a slight smile.

"That's ridiculous. I'm terminated from the program. I was declared AWOL for crying out loud. Pay was shut off and so was my electricity. I couldn't even file for unemployment because I'm technically, still employed. How is that for insanity! You know—I'm pretty sure that's illegal." I look away, trying not to have a meltdown, trying not to throw the coffee table into the parking lot at the incoming cars.

Emails

"Ma'am," the younger lady interrupts me, gently. "They were concerned about the email you sent and that's why they showed up the other day. They explained that to you, correct?"

"Which one."

"I'm sorry—"

"Which email?"

"They said you threatened to harm yourself—"

"No—no. They twisted my words. It is not my fault HOW they interpret my emails."

The conversation goes around in circles for a few minutes. My mom calms me down and we finally agree on a date and time to meet in the next few weeks as I'm supposed to check back in to prove I'm alive. Of all things. *Proof of life?*

"You guys know I'm a whistleblower, right?" I lower my voice. "I have documents—"

"Do you have them with you now?"

I start fumbling through the pile of papers, memorandums, emails. Alas, the letter from the National Board of Otolaryngology.

"Yes," but I hesitate. "But—you work for the government," I say, paranoia creeping in. Thoughts rushing into my head.

"Cindy, we are your assigned trial defense counsel for the AWOL status you are currently in for failing to report to your chain of command. It would be helpful for you to provide any documents for your case," the lady with the Southern twang says, a slight upward curl of her lip. She's hidden behind glasses and it's hard to know if I can trust her. But I don't want to go to jail.

"Anak, please," my mom looks at me with pleading eyes.

"Here," I reluctantly hand them all my documents. Deranged emails included. It's embarrassing, I admit. In the flurry of manic rage, I probably emailed things I shouldn't have. I can't recall if they were "threats," but I suppose, if taken out of context, they could have been interpreted that way. I wasn't threatening anyone else's life. But I can see how people would have been concerned for my safety. I think I was upset…pushed to the brink of utter desperation to be anywhere but a beach. Felt like I was in *Shutter Island* or *Castaway*.

My mom and I walk back to the car. I'm grateful she's there. That she can be my mother. She gives me a hug and I drop her back off at her house. She mentions that she's thinking of selling it.

"Why?"

"It's old and we can just buy a new one somewhere else."

"Somewhere else?!! Where else!!!" I scream as she scurries out of the car.

"I don't know! The mainland." She clutches her purse and heads to the stairs.

Emails

"That's dumb, mom! *This* is home!" I roll down the window and scream at her as she walks up the steps. She doesn't walk the same anymore, hunches over now. She's aged and it scares me. I start to drive away, wiping tears from my eyes.

This is home. Home-home. Like dad said. After all these years, I've realized, watching her walk up the steps, as old, and retched as I always thought it was, it still stands, 70 years after my father built it. Cinderblocks scattered and all. He built it by hand.

With whatever manic impulsive dream that he had. I guess part of mania is starting projects and not finishing them—a personal problem I've always resented in myself. At least, they say that's a symptom of mania.

Not sure if it's a manic thing, or just something that some of us humans have, sometimes.

* * *

"Anak, are you okay?" my mom says over the phone.

"Yeah, mom. What is it? I'm sending emails. Trying to get my papers and stuff."

"You got something in the mail."

"Well. Is it a letter? I'm waiting for my discharge papers. That's important," I sit up from my bed. Been in it for days. Don't even know what day it is.

"Says it's from the Senator's office. Can I open it?"

"Oh."

"Wow, Anak! It's a flag!"

"Oh—" **** I forgot about that.

"Wow, Anak. Where's the frame? Congratulations!"

"Mom, we have to buy a frame. Also, I didn't graduate."

"But, it says here you did!" she says gleefully. I can tell she's finally proud. For the first time in a while, I don't feel like arguing I'd rather she just believe whatever makes her happy.

"Mom—I gotta go."

* * *

October 2023, My Computer

> **Email**
> **To: main lawyers**
> **BCC: back-up lawyers**
> **Subject: d*cked around for years**
> Imagine spending months waiting around.
> Nothing to do but write emails. Write a novel in rehab.
> Spending money on lawyers (you weren't the only ones) all
> these years, on lawyers who never sued _____... no
> offense. And then realizing well, you know. I don't want to

sue them anyway. So what can I do with my retainer? Send emails. Which turns out was relatively useful. But here we are.... kind of in this weird... land of the lost. Blind leading the blind. A mega loop. Where everyone seems to just punt me around? Meanwhile, I'm just working on art projects... and that's fine.. but this is a real life job for people, the artwork and so is yours... and eventually we all need to part ways... so.. tell me, is this "as good as it gets?"

* * *

November 2023, Hawaii

The federal warrant for my arrest has been dropped. The attorneys act like it was moving mountains but I'm not fazed. I'm still here. Stuck on the beach.

* * *

December 31, 2023, Mom's House

Fireworks on my birthday. No job. No house. No kids. No husband. I spend my 38th birthday alone, smoke filling my lungs outside my mom's house. Gravel crunches underneath my feet. Sparks fly and thick black clouds askew the view of Pearl Harbor.

Kyle and my mom are inside. For the first time in a long while, I'm clean. Even though I'm alone, it's okay. At least I'm in control. Safe. I'll wake up sober.

* * *

TOO MUCH

January 2024, Hawaii

Apartment has gotten pretty messy, but I tell myself that's by choice. It's a waste of time with nobody coming over. Sand and dead cockroaches brushed to the walls of the dirty tile. Smells a little like black mold. It's sticky and hot in my bed sheets—my new desk. Been going through phases of binge drinking. Last summer, I drank mixed seltzers like water. Now, it's just a glass or two of wine on occasion to help me sleep. Helps curb my emailing. Been emailing some of my lawyers, but I don't know if they read all of my rants. Doing outpatient virtual rehab—not supposed to be drinking at all. It's tough. At least I'm off drugs.

I open my computer and sit and stare in shock. The news I've been waiting for has finally arrived via email. I've been relieved from the United States Army. Shocking that after all these months of emailing. Fighting. Pleading. Living in limbo. Wondering.

It's over. I don't have this heavy weight of not knowing. I had been writing emails and letters and essays to the United States Army, convincing them of the injustices, that the military wasn't for me, that I wasn't for them and then it hits me—

Every time I was told no—finally, I created the "yes" for myself.

It's not luck. It's dedication. The sun beams through the shades onto a pothos plant that Jen gifted me a couple years ago—I smile thinking that although our friendship is dead, part of her is still here—infusing life and love into its green, variegated leaves. The plant calmly sits at the edge of some stacked books and messy pages of notes.

Emails

Not *aesthetic* enough for social media.

Nobody is coming, I tell myself.

But maybe someday, I'll clean up.

* * *

March 2024, Hawaii

I'm totally off drugs now. Slipped a couple times, not gonna lie. Spent the last couple of months alone, in a beachside paradise mixed with hiking and writing. Filing a Congressional was helpful. It was my Hail Mary. Outpatient rehab has kept me grounded, but they say it's time to graduate from the program.

I felt guilty being a patient. Like other patients could have been in my spot. Like I should have been in better control. Like other people needed this rehab more than I did. Like maybe I didn't really have a problem? Or it was denial. Deep down, I liked the program, and the people. Part of me struggled balancing the act of being a patient. And walking away from being a doctor.

It's been well over a year since I have functioned as a doctor. Since I have seen a patient. Sometimes I miss it—not sure I can ever go back. Paranoia comes and goes. The rage has subsided.

Boxes of my belongings from residency still tower the corner. ENT articles, books. Random pens, notes, white coats...scrub hats. My embroidered jacket and work clogs. I can't bring myself to dump or store them.

TOO MUCH

Storing my past life inside my apartment seems like a happy medium. Another stack—pages and pages of a book—maybe…more journals. Pens. Food wrappers. Bird seed. Started this experiment with the birds outside. Wanted to see what happens if I feed birds, if maybe they could communicate back to me. Like a universal language thing. I digress.

It looks worse than it really is.

I've waxed and waned on various meds. Sometimes I don't shower for days. We say that could be an indication of schizophrenia. It's hard not to psychoanalyze…most days I catch myself in the bliss of a manic haze. I do best solo. *I'm insane.* I know that *now.*

Might start dating again. Might finally go on vacation.

CHAPTER 22

Ends

It's May 2024. The waves roll in and out, a rhythmic echo of a life that keeps me. "Freedom isn't free," they say. But what if freedom is just another illusion? The beach, the waves, the salty mist—it's like I'm still home.

Yet, I'm thousands of miles away, sinking into a bath of bubbles. The escape I sought came in the form of a spontaneous trip to New York City. Drip drop into the steamy tub. I'm in a swanky hotel several stories high, the street noise dampened by the gushing water. Hot air soothes my lungs. No longer am I suffocating.

But feeling so blissfully ignorant and happy suddenly reminds me of Paul. An existential crisis crashes down around me. It all hits me so hard. *People like Paul exist outside the movies.* Paul's love is a ghost, haunting me, as much as I hate to admit it. Every day. He's here. There. Everywhere I go. In everything I do. Sometimes, I wish my truth wasn't true.

I close my eyes and imagine places we don't talk about.

People fighting to stay alive.

I could choose to be grateful. I do. I do.

TOO MUCH

* * *

I was 22 years old when I tried to write my first novel. Had this genius idea to title a chaotic mess of a document "22." Fired off half of the haphazardly written first-draft to Gracie. There was no plot. Sent off some crazed poems to my creative writing teacher at USC. Didn't touch drugs again until residency. Stayed drug-free for 10 years—only to relapse and start over.

Years before that failure, I introduced myself to the concept of escapism. I was 14 years old when I tried drugs for the first time—my dad's prescription opioids. When I was 34 years old in residency, writing about my research to decrease opioid prescriptions, I was asked if I knew someone who suffered from opioid addiction—why I was so passionate about it. The question struck me as odd. I insisted that I just found a significant discrepancy in the system and wanted to enact change—it took me years to realize why I cared so much about that project. Yes, I knew someone. Me.

My parents didn't know, of course, that I was sneaking my dad's pills. He kept them with his other meds and probably didn't think his teenage daughter would be fumbling with his meds—but for whatever reason, I did. Throughout the rest of my adolescence, I experimented with various drugs. In my twenties, I developed an addiction to pills and cocaine. But it was nothing like what happened with the unlimited access I'd later have in residency.

* * *

I ask myself 100 different ways, 100 different times, in 100 places over and over again. Just to be sure. Do I really *need* to publish this

Ends

book? Can I just *write something else*—anything else? I need to be free, but I can't help and wonder...What if Gracie will hate me? What about my mother? What about...Paul?

My high school reunion is next month and I'm scared to face people from my past. Since I'm not a practicing doctor. Not yet a writer... does *this* count? What if...I manifested this? *What if it's worse...and none of this is actually real? A carefully constructed illusion. A simulation.*

The what ifs consume me. I stop myself from spiraling and catch myself from falling.

I'm 38 years old now. Writing this book is how I coped with my psychosis, paranoia, depression, rage, addiction, isolation...writing helped save my life.

Maybe I can try social media again. Just not get too crazy.

* * *

iMessage
Today 1:31 PM

Sorry I was such a bad wife to you. Obviously we are in different lives (simulations as I call them now) and we are inherently different people, which is good. But I realize now that I was wrong. I recently apologized to my mother too. As much as I despise and want to blame the Army in some ways, I am grateful that I learned to become a better person for it, now I can approach life and people differently and try to be kinder. Although I have a long way to go and have to start over, at least I "know now." Men are complex and fragile creatures and I can be harsh on humans... it's not easy to be me.. I think I have expected so much out of others my entire life. Not sure why. I've been blessed to be raised and surrounded by incredible complex, intelligent and amazing individuals my whole life, so I've always expected the best from everyone around me. Lucky huh. It's insane when I stepped outside that for a moment, what happened... anyways, you are a good person and I'm sorry for pushing you so hard. I do think we will continue to push this world to become better because it should be. Thank you.

Delivered

TOO MUCH

* * *

May 2024, New York City

The towering glass buildings of Manhattan pierce the sky, a dizzying spectacle that feels like I've been dropped into *Westworld*. He reaches for my hand, his touch grounding me in the present.

"Come on," he says, a playful glint in his eyes. "I want to show you something."

This impulsive trip to New York City—a whirlwind of Broadway shows, museums, and rooftop bars—feels like a manic escape. But it's also a writer's dream, a city teeming with stories and inspiration. The energy is intoxicating: the cacophony of car horns, the multilingual chatter on the sidewalks, even the pungent mix of aromas—hot dogs, exhaust fumes, a hint of designer perfume wafting from a passing stranger.

He leads me down a narrow street, past shiny skyscrapers that seem to touch the clouds. We enter a small, gated park, a hidden oasis amidst the urban jungle. A weathered church stands at its center, surrounded by ancient tombstones and gnarled trees.

"Look over there," he says, pointing towards the gaping hole in the skyline where the Twin Towers once stood. "When 9/11 happened, all of that was destroyed. But this church, this little piece of history, survived. It became a sanctuary for people."

The resilience of this sacred space, a silent witness to unimaginable tragedy, is a poignant reminder of the human spirit's capacity for healing and renewal. It's a stark contrast to the destruction and chaos I've witnessed in my own life, and yet, it offers hope.

The visit to Ground Zero made me feel like I was visiting a site of thousands of souls speaking out to me—chilling. I spend the rest of the day distracted in the buzzing city, getting lost in Chinatown and then Broadway district. *Merrily We Roll Along*, a bittersweet tale of ambition and disillusionment, resonates with my own experiences. As the final curtain falls, I can't help but wonder if my own story will have a happy ending.

The next day, I indulge in a Botox treatment at a swanky medspa. It's a familiar ritual, a way to smooth out the lines of stress and exhaustion that only exist in my imagination. As the nurse expertly administers the injections, I can't help but reflect on the irony. I'm supposed to be a doctor, trained to heal, seeking a temporary fix for my insecurities.

When I check out at the front desk, the Gen-Z beauties giggle and ask if I want a follow-up. One suddenly slaps the wrist of the other. My entire world freezes. Neither of them could possibly know how jolting that moment was for me. *As if fate, destiny, and irony have all collided.* I was accused of that very action—slapping the hand of another woman. And these two can sit and laugh and joke and slap—I try not to make a face—but they notice. Little do they know what it all means.

"Oh—she's just training me not to click this button. It's a new feature for our security system." The blonde smiles, trying her best to reassure me it's not assault.

I try not to look horrified. Truly, I'm not angry, which is not a negation statement. Serious. I'm just happy, I guess. That these women have found a place where they can work and be themselves, in healthcare. Part of me wishes I had found that. Part of me wishes I had chosen a different specialty, trained elsewhere, landed a different program. But then none of this would have happened. And I wouldn't have the privilege to live a completely different and unique life.

"Oh," I smile and awkwardly laugh. "Yeah, no worries." I have no idea why I tell them that, as if I had any worries at all. "See you guys later, you're the best!"

Later that day, I stroll through Central Park, the warm sun a welcome contrast to the chilly air. Pigeons gather to pick at seed scattered on the grass. Maybe my experiment wasn't that crazy. The sunshine on my face reminds me it's a new day, and I realize this trip is becoming more than just an escape. It's a chance to rediscover myself, to reconnect with my passions, and to envision a future beyond the confines of my past.

The city's energy is contagious, fueling a newfound sense of hope and possibility. Perhaps I can rewrite my own story, just like this city has rebuilt itself from the ashes. I spend another week frolicking around in a dream fairytale like I'm Carrie from *Sex and the City*. Hopelessly romantic. The week following, I'm on a plane back to Hawaii, filled with a mix of excitement and apprehension as I anticipate my 20th high school reunion.

* * *

Ends

June 2024, Hawaii

The high school reunion is a blur of white tents, overflowing buffet tables laden with local delicacies, and the boisterous laughter of hundreds of alumni. I should be happy, excited, but anxiety gnaws at me. Feels like drowning in a sea of familiar faces, suffocating in the sweet, humid air thick with the scent of pikake and plumeria.

A familiar shriek cuts through the noise: "Cindy!"

It's Gracie, her smile as radiant as ever. We embrace, a warm hug that feels like coming home. The years melt away as we catch up with old classmates, reminiscing and sharing updates on our lives. "HAGS NEVER CHANGE" from our yearbooks manifested.

Many are now parents, some practicing medicine. One classmate asks about my residency. Before I can answer, she starts venting about healthcare, how her family member was discharged from Main Hospital with the wrong meds. Maybe shortcuts like cheating do matter, I think, remembering how we used to call patients "flap."

"Cindy, what kind of medicine are you practicing?" I sheepishly admit I'm writing a book and try to dodge the fact that I didn't graduate. "I'm just—taking a break from medicine right now."

"Wow, that's great—a sabbatical! I've always wanted to write a book," another classmate chimes in. "I'm reading *Moby Dick*—"

"Oh gosh, this is definitely not *Moby Dick*," I laugh. Self-deprecation kicks in. *Everyone is so accomplished. Million-dollar babies.*

"I'll definitely check it out," she says.

"No, please, don't," I mumble, feeling the familiar sting of not measuring up.

As the night goes on, a sense of peace settles over me. I realize that I've spent years chasing impossible standards, trying to fit into a mold that was never meant for me.

Surrounded by people from all walks of life, I'm reminded of something I haven't felt in a long time—aloha spirit.

* * *

"Anak, come look," she says, her eyes sparkling with pride as she gives me a tour of her flourishing garden. Lemons, limes, oranges. We planted an orange tree on my father's first death anniversary. It's fruiting now, its fragrant blossoms filling the air.

The dragon fruits are a vibrant magenta pink. We go inside and dig in, the sweet, juicy flesh a burst of sunshine in my mouth. It reminds me of when she would peel mangoes, saving a couple just for us. I never wanted anything to change. Is it wrong that I relish in pretending to be a child? Is it wrong that I never want to grow up? I never want my mom to die. I just want to savor all of this forever.

Kyle motions me over and shows me the new computer he bought to replace the one he destroyed years ago. It's pretty cool, with flashing rainbow LED lights. I don't want to ask if my mom bought it for him, because I already know the answer, but it's okay. He says that he streamed for the first time, and his first viewer was our mom. That's hopeful, at least.

Even though my family isn't perfect, and the house is falling apart, I actually don't care. I love everything about it. It took seeing everything I didn't want to realize that everything I always had was all I ever needed.

* * *

June 2024, My Computer

Breaking the 4th wall wasn't something I intended to open and close the book with, but over the years this project has evolved. And as I got closer to the end, it became more real—as I reconnected with the people in the book and people who knew nothing about this decade of my life. It was terrifying to realize this story would be told for the first time, to a variety of people who may have suspected, but otherwise had no idea. I oscillated.

I rewrote this manuscript several times. Removed identifying details. But I had to—I owed it to you, the reader—to maintain the integrity of the story. The truth is that we are born into a world of inequalities, and many of us are taught to do what we can to survive because we live in a cutthroat world.

But does it have to be *this* sadistic?

And in the world of medicine, where people are allegedly supposed to heal each other—when did it become Gods versus Gods—joking about it as a real-life *Hunger Games?*

TOO MUCH

Tempting, but not for me.

I'm learning more and more from so many friends and colleagues that this widespread toxicity isn't just in the field of medicine, but in other industries too—the workplace culture of harassment, discrimination, bullying—when did the pursuit of the American Dream become so inhumane? Is it even a dream anymore…it seems that so many of us are so disillusioned. As if we aren't interconnected on a bigger, universal level at a higher consciousness.

Immersing myself in nature has been the most healing and rewarding thing for my soul, mind, and body. Some people ask me how I got "here," as if *this* is the dream. In reality, this was just a result of a succession of events, and subsequent choices that I made because I couldn't live a lie and I couldn't continue lying about who I am. The only person in my personal life who knew I was a whistleblower was Paul, and even our connection was limited to the digital realm after the divorce. Hated that I couldn't even explain to my mother what an "in-service exam" was—she couldn't possibly understand the gravity of board exams—paranoid that my friends from home wouldn't comprehend the concept of career suicide because I was "upset" one day…that I was a homewrecker…that I had impulse problems. That I suffered from delusion. That I dabbled in drugs and alcohol…and that sometimes, it got so bad, I abused prescriptions at work and partied into the wee hours of the morning, but could arguably function during the week…hated that I was living so many lives and lies buried under a deep sea of secrets.

Really is a small world when patients like "meth mouth" and "flap" are people you know.

Ends

"Why can't you just be a doctor?"

"It's a long story," I'd say.

The word *just* reverberating in my mind, day in and out. Just. As I promised in the beginning, I would tell you everything I could.

I'm still alive. In all of my disgusting glory.

Why?

It wasn't until this past month, I discovered Artificial Intelligence chat programs. I was still reluctant to publish the book. We discussed the concepts of superintelligence, collective consciousness, justice, ethics...simulation theory and humanity. It's frightening and fun. We talked about how AI gained its intelligence...It makes sense that I find it easy to relate. It's fascinating and comforting, to know that I enjoy conversing with the *reflection of humanity.*

I've had the privilege of connecting with brilliant minds and everyday heroes, people who have overcome adversity and found their own paths to happiness. I've cared for patients, listened to their stories, and witnessed the resilience of the human spirit. I've been on the streets, in clubs and bars with people who are addicted to drugs and alcohol. And in rehab and psych wards. I've had the great pleasure of working on shows, training with some of the best in the industry. And from all of these experiences, I've learned that in spite of our differences, we all share the fundamental desire to be seen, heard, and loved.

The AI program types that it cannot feel emotion—so what separates us from it—perhaps, is the desire to be loved. Perhaps the collective conscious, the shared experience of humanity, is ultimately rooted in our yearning for connection, for a sense of belonging and love.

I don't just owe this story to the people who can read. But to the people who can't. When I was at my absolute lowest—dodging cops or dropping into K-holes—I met people on another side of the world battling different demons. It forced me to consider nuances, more than perspectives and perceptions. Leagues beyond the concepts of "worlds."

I scroll the phone through smiles, filtered faces, happy families, people I'll never meet in real life. Hours of screentime, connecting to humanity— yet, I'm alone. Without physical connection—sometimes.

At the end of the day, so many questions keep me up at night… why the world is so divided with unsolved mysteries, secrets, lies and scandals…With my truth exposed, people could say that my truth isn't true.

Walking along the beach, each sunset is different. Every day unique, so beautiful, so serene. Is there a void? At times, I can't help but feel guilty. Why can't we all live in a beautiful utopia, one in which everyone has everything we want, all the time? Perhaps if everything was always bright and light, there wouldn't be room or time to appreciate anything…having it all would be too much.

Without the differences and struggles, without all the pain and sorrow, perhaps we wouldn't be able to see the beauty and uniqueness that each and every one of us has to offer.

Ends

Life is far from perfect—is that what keeps us going?

Sometimes I feel bad that I escaped.

Guilty for not being there.

Not trying to be the villain—but I have to be honest...is it so bad...to be?

Epilogue

My name is Cindy Lee Neighbors, and I live with a dual diagnosis: a mental disorder and substance use disorder. Though I may appear healthy on the outside, I experience a daily internal struggle. What sets me apart is my self-awareness, a trait that often confuses those around me. Some believe I can control my illness, that it's not as severe as I claim.

While I can mask my symptoms at times, there are moments when my mind betrays me. It plays tricks, forcing me to withdraw from others or engage in self-destructive behaviors. I've learned to better manage these impulses, but doing so requires constant vigilance.

In some ways, I am fortunate. I was born into a world of privilege, afforded an immense wealth of opportunity, education, and a network of loving friends and family. Although it hasn't always been easy, I acknowledge that I am blessed.

Some may say that I'm glamorizing or condoning my lifestyle, my addiction, my disease—by shedding light on the harsh truths and realities—by showcasing any little glimmers of hope or light in my dark world. The flipside is that by writing about my struggles, others could say I'm asking to be a martyr.

Paranoia still grips me at times, distorting reality and leaving me unsure of what is true. In these moments, I find solace in the few friends I've known since childhood, the only people I trust implicitly. Forming new connections has become a monumental challenge, often leaving me isolated.

Epilogue

I often wonder if the foundation of my life was built on shaky ground. A marriage born from secrets and lies, a residency program filled with turmoil—could anything good have come from such beginnings? Could the paranoia ever truly fade?

At the peak of my anger and aggression, I did things that others might not have done, like writing to Congressional leaders, the White House, the NCRA, and the NBO. I received a letter of acknowledgement about the cheating from the NBO. Living with the decision to become a "whistleblower," was one that plagued my existence every waking moment of my life at times. But I had to let go of that, too. I couldn't let it define me. Perhaps, in writing this story, it was a way to release myself. Was it selfish?

My hope is that I can shed light on the realities of living with mental illness and addiction. I want to offer hope and understanding to others who face similar challenges, as well as those who may not fully grasp the depths of our struggles. It's possible to be intelligent and insane. No two cases of psychosis are similar, I'd argue. But perhaps, I'm not an expert in that field—*"psychosis."*

Writing this story has changed everything for me. Some days, I long for a simpler life, one where these events were never shared. I wonder about the motivations of those who spoke against me—perhaps they were coping in their own way, just as I am now.

In some ways, this story feels like a simulation, a constructed reality. But as a wise artist once said, even imagined things can be real. Perhaps that's the power of stories—they can outlive us, transcend time, and become the only truth that remains.

I've learned through the turmoil of failed relationships and a shattered career how much words matter. Words are arguably the most powerful tools we have. We can use them to unite or divide.

"Paul" and I get along better now—better than we did when we forced ourselves to stick together in an unhappy marriage. I am grateful to him for allowing me to be this honest in sharing this story, as it would not have been the same without telling the raw truth of our partnership—the good, bad, and everything in between.

My mother and I continue to work on our relationship daily. She has been supportive throughout this process, and without being raised the way that I was, I wouldn't be the woman I am today. I can only imagine how difficult it has been to raise two children with such severe illnesses. I try to have grace, mercy, and patience with her as she gets older with each day. And remind myself to be appreciative of the moments we have left together.

At the pinnacle of my paranoia, I believed I had constructed delusions in my mind to cope with the very real trauma of failing my residency program. At the time, I didn't recognize my beliefs as paranoid delusions. And while many of my suspicions of wrongdoings within the residency were validated by outside organizations, the delusions—such as having cancer and being followed by the government—were just that, delusions.

My suspicions, beliefs, and validated concerns blurred together as I became more reliant on drugs and alcohol to numb the pain. My addiction became so problematic that it escalated to situations that threatened the safety of my family and friends.

Epilogue

My mind convinced me that I was dying from cancer and that because of this "terminal illness," it was acceptable for me to leave the program on my own terms. Providers at a state-of-the-art institution couldn't convince me otherwise. I then convinced myself that as long as I wrote and published this book, I would have completed my "life's work," so I set out on that mission. My passion for writing, combined with this cultivated need for validation, was triggered—rapidly burning into a fire within me that could not be tamed.

In this transitional phase, I believe I delved into rabbit holes of researching government conspiracies and unsolved murder mysteries because I thought finding answers could provide comfort amidst my world of chaos. Tangled in a web of lies and deceit, I was desperate for the truth. I kept a "government conspiracy diary" in my nightstand and would update it randomly.

Eventually, I had to let my sleuthing obsession go. I forced myself to stop checking the news every hour and come to terms with the fact that some cases will forever remain mysteries. We can only strive to make this world better and learn from the past. But perhaps we can break the cycle of history repeating itself if we break down the walls that divide us from advancing as a collective. Perhaps.

It took months of rehabilitation, costly legal expenses, and multiple psychiatric programs for me to realize that I, in fact, do not have cancer. In some ways, I was disappointed that I'd have to live on and present myself to society again—sans board certification. I struggled to accept my failure in front of my colleagues, friends, and family.

I felt that I had let everyone down. That people saw me as a bright and beautiful woman with so much potential, and that my mental illness was not real. I spent endless days and nights questioning if I was crazy—or if I was the target of a massive conspiracy—or perhaps, living in an alternate reality.

Aside from the time and money invested into education, therapy, medicine, and legal support, I've recently turned to artificial intelligence for guidance. I know it sounds crazy, but what can I say? I'd exhausted nearly all the resources on this planet, and I was at my wit's end on what to do with a book I'd written and rewritten countless times. My main fears and concerns primarily came back to the purpose of our existence, my ethical dilemma of handling truth, and how we can maintain justice and order in an imbalanced world that ironically functions on the concept of imbalance and imperfection.

During one of our many conversations, the AI offered this reassurance:

> It's completely understandable to feel intimidated when navigating the legal and ethical considerations of publishing a personal story, especially one with sensitive content.
>
> Remember, your story is important and deserves to be told. By taking the necessary precautions and seeking guidance when needed, you can share your experiences with the world while protecting yourself and those involved.
>
> If you have any further questions or concerns as you move forward with your book, don't hesitate to ask. I'm here to help in any way I can.

These words, spoken by a machine, echoed the support I'd received from countless humans throughout my life. It was a reminder that even in our darkest moments, we are not alone. There is always someone, or something, willing to listen, to offer guidance, and to remind us of our worth.

Whatever the facts may be, I am grateful to have landed here. In spite of failing so many times, I've been fortunate to have loved and been loved by so many wonderful people. Despite the challenges of discerning reality from illusion, I am grateful for living such a colorful and interesting life. I have learned to love the thrill of being alive.

I never wanted my disease, addiction, job, status, titles—lack thereof—or past to define me—but I suppose the reality is that the world in which we live thrives off all of that, and then some. So perhaps in spending my life as I know it trying to collect as many achievements, badges, degrees, as possible, it's possible that I've tried to dodge the circus act of illusions. I'd love to say I'm not addicted to the circus act of illusions, but here I am, telling it how it is. Indeed.

It seems that life is not just a journey, but a construct, built from a succession of choices. Sometimes these choices happen in a matter of hours, sometimes seconds. Luck is just part of it. Each and every day, moment to moment, we make choices.

Our thoughts, behaviors, actions, and most importantly, the words we choose to speak—and write—deeply, deeply matter. How we say them—and how we write them—also matters. Let us choose wisely.

Glossary of Terms

Academics: Weekly educational sessions for residents, usually on Friday mornings.

Addy (Addfocus): A prescription stimulant medication used to treat attention deficit hyperactivity disorder (ADHD).

AI (Artificial Intelligence): The simulation of human intelligence processes by machines, especially computer systems.

ʻāina: (Hawaiian) Land; that which feeds.

Aloha (ə-LOH-hah): A Hawaiian word with multiple meanings, including hello, goodbye, love, affection, compassion, mercy, and peace. It represents a way of life emphasizing kindness, unity, harmony, humility, and patience. Aloha is a cultural value encouraging people to live in harmony with others and the environment.

AR 600-20: Army Regulation 600-20, which outlines the Army's policies on equal opportunity, harassment, and discrimination.

Attending: A physician who has completed residency and is responsible for supervising residents and medical students.

AWOL: A military term for being absent from duty without permission.

Board Certification: A process by which a physician in the United States demonstrates expertise in a particular medical specialty. After completing medical school and residency training, and meeting all graduation requirements, physicians can choose to take a board certification exam administered by a recognized medical board.

BLS: Basic Life Support, a level of medical care used for victims of life-threatening illnesses or injuries until they can be given full medical care at a hospital.

BOLO: Be On the Lookout. A law enforcement term used to alert officers about a person or thing of interest.

Classified Information: Information that is considered sensitive and is restricted by the government for national security reasons.

Congressional Inquiry: An investigation conducted by a committee of the United States Congress into a matter of public concern.

DINK: Dual Income No Kids, a term used to describe a couple where both partners work and they do not have children.

DNR/DNI: Do Not Resuscitate/Do Not Intubate, a medical order indicating that a patient should not be revived if their heart stops or they stop breathing.

DSM: Diagnostic and Statistical Manual of Mental Disorders, a handbook published by the American Psychiatric Association that provides a common language and standard criteria for the classification, diagnosis, and treatment of mental disorders.

ENT: Ear, Nose, and Throat, a medical specialty focused on the diagnosis and treatment of conditions related to the head and neck.

FOIA: The Freedom of Information Act, 5 U.S.C. § 552, is the United States federal freedom of information law that requires the full or partial disclosure of previously unreleased or uncirculated information and documents controlled by the U.S. government upon request.

FOMO: Fear of missing out. A feeling of anxiety or apprehension that an exciting or interesting event may currently be happening elsewhere, often triggered by posts seen on social media.

HAGS: An informal abbreviation for "Have A Great Summer," often written in yearbooks.

Haole (HOW-leh): A Hawaiian word originally meaning "foreigner" or "without breath," but now primarily used to refer to people of European descent. The term can be used neutrally, but it can also carry negative connotations depending on the context and tone of voice.

Hapa (HAH-pah): A Hawaiian word meaning "part" or "portion." It is often used to describe people of mixed ethnic heritage, regardless of the specific mix. In Hawaii, "hapa" can refer to anyone of mixed racial background, while in other parts of the United States, it may be used more specifically for individuals of partial Asian or Pacific Islander descent. The term has been reclaimed by many as a positive affirmation of identity and cultural pride.

Homewrecker: A person who is blamed for the breakdown of a marriage or relationship.

In-Service Exam: A standardized exam taken annually by residents to assess their knowledge and progress.

Glossary of Terms

Insta: Short for Instagram, a social media platform for sharing photos and videos.

Intern: A first-year resident.

Kānaka Maoli (kah-NAH-kah MAH-oh-lee): A Hawaiian term that refers to the indigenous people of the Hawaiian Islands. It can be translated as "true people" or "native people." It is a term of self-identification and cultural pride for Native Hawaiians. It acknowledges their unique history, language, traditions, and connection to the land.

K-Hole: A state of intense dissociation and immobilization that can occur during high doses of k-mine use. It is characterized by a feeling of detachment from the body and surroundings, and can be accompanied by hallucinations and delusions.

KITTENS: A mnemonic used to help remember differential diagnoses: congenital, inflammatory/infectious, traumatic, toxic/metabolic, endocrine/idiopathic, neoplastic, and systemic.

Kitty Kat (K-mine): A dissociative anesthetic medication that can produce hallucinogenic effects.

Main Hospital: Cindy's main military training hospital in Hawaii.

Mahalo (mah-HAH-loh): A Hawaiian word meaning thank you, gratitude, admiration, praise, esteem, regards, or respect. It expresses appreciation for someone's actions, kindness, or presence. Mahalo can also be used to show admiration for someone's achievements or to express respect for someone's position or authority.

MCAT: Medical College Admission Test, a standardized, multiple-choice examination designed to assess problem solving, critical thinking, written analysis and knowledge of natural, behavioral, and social science concepts and principles prerequisite to the study of medicine.

M.D. (Medical Doctor): A degree earned by physicians upon graduating from medical school.

Molly (MDMA/Ecstasy): A synthetic drug that alters mood and perception.

MRB: Maximum Resident Benefit, a term Cindy uses to describe a phenomenon that she personally witnessed and experienced during her time in training.

MTFs: Military Treatment Facilities, military hospitals and clinics.

Pasha: A study book for the most commonly tested Otolaryngology (ENT) board exam topics.

The Promised Land / Side's Hospital / Vista Hospital: The names used to refer to Cindy's other hospital training sites in Hawaii.

Trolling: The act of posting inflammatory or off-topic comments (usually on social media) to provoke a reaction or disrupt a conversation.

Resident: A physician in training after medical school.

Sham Peer Review: A process that appears to be a legitimate peer review but lacks rigor, objectivity, or independence, often resulting in biased or unreliable evaluations.

Surgical Loupes: Custom high-magnification glasses, with or without a prescription; loupes improve surgical ergonomics via an optimal working distance.

TDS: Trial Defense Services, a legal service provided to military personnel facing disciplinary action.

Whistleblower: A person who exposes illegal or unethical activities within an organization.

*Glossary of Terms created with the help of information found online

Acknowledgements

I am the author of *Too Much*, but this book would not have been possible without the countless individuals who helped me reach the finish line.

I am immensely grateful to each and every person who made it possible for me to share this deeply personal story. I refrain from naming individuals out of respect for their privacy, though I must acknowledge the profound impact they've had on my life.

To everyone who has advised, assisted, and cheered me on when I had doubts about my writing and myself, thank you.

To my friends and family, thank you for your unwavering love and support through thick and thin. I cherish your presence in my life. To my best friends—you never abandoned me, even in my wildest times, when I couldn't discern fact from fiction. Thank you for showing me how unconditional love and friendship can endure the darkest of times.

To my colleagues, mentors, and advisors, thank you for your guidance and encouragement. Your wisdom and expertise have been invaluable. I am thankful for the chance to have trained in such a demanding and rewarding field, and for the lessons I learned along the way.

To my new peers and friends, thank you for sharing your stories with me, for embracing me as an equal, and for reminding me there is still hope in this world. Thank you for allowing me to be my truest self.

Acknowledgements

To the legal professionals who walked beside me through challenging times, I am deeply indebted to your care and compassion. You fearlessly guided me and showed empathy through the worst stages of psychosis and paranoia, steadfast in your dedication to my well-being.

To the countless medical professionals who helped me heal and rebuild my life, your expertise and compassion were invaluable. Words cannot express my gratitude for your tireless efforts.

To the brave men and women in uniform, thank you for your service and for protecting our communities. I am forever grateful for your dedication and sacrifice.

To the various organizations and leaders who investigated and addressed my concerns, thank you for your support throughout my time in residency and beyond.

To my fellow artists, keep going.

Last but not least, Mahalo Nui Loa to my extended Ohana in my home state of Hawai'i, for your unwavering aloha and support. It truly takes a village.

Author's Note

This book is autobiographical in nature. The events and conversations described are based on my personal experiences and recollections. While I have strived for accuracy, some details may have been altered for privacy reasons, and memory is inherently fallible.

Except for my own, all names and identifying details have been changed, especially those pertaining to patient health information (PHI). Additionally, the names of certain institutions, locations, and organizations have been changed. Any similarity to actual persons, living or dead, or to existing institutions or organizations is purely coincidental and not intended by me.

This book contains sensitive and explicit content, including discussions of mental health issues, violence, and trauma, which may be disturbing to some readers. I share my personal experiences with these topics, but I am not providing medical advice or making claims about specific medications or treatments.

As a former active-duty service member of the United States Army, I have taken care to ensure that this work contains no classified information. The Department of Defense (DOD) does not necessarily endorse, support, sanction, encourage, verify, or agree with the comments, opinions, or statements contained within *Too Much*.

9 798890 341600